Mission

amidst Crisis

Society of African Missions

2021 – Rome

Mission amidst Crisis, Bulletin No. 153

© 2021 SMA publications
Cover picture by Anna Shvets, www.pexels.com
All rights reserved

ISBN: 9798731274180

Previous Bulletins

SMA publications
Società delle missioni africane
Via della Nocetta, 111, Roma 00164, Italia

www.smainternational.info
media@ smainternational.org

Table of Contents

Spotlight

Editorial

Missionaries stay indoors, pious Christians kneel in front of televisions and sanitizers replace the Holy Water!!! Many things we thought impossible have become the new normal due to the COVID-19 pandemic. As people change their plans, they discover that they must also let go part of their lifestyle and many of their popular beliefs. Some find the experience overwhelming and the others eye-opening.

This bulletin, on the one hand gives voice to our numerous pains, confusions, and anxieties and on the other hand attempts to make this pandemic a steppingstone and a springboard for a better future. We have three sections: Roots, Vision and Spotlight.

Roots

When you face a new challenge like banking through a mobile device or buying your first sanitizer, you seek advice from someone who has already done it. Our humanity has seen major crises. As we are going through the present pandemic, we look at the history to see how people lived challenging times and what we can learn from their experiences.

The devastating Second World War has thoroughly reshaped the world. With the help of Dr. Roberta Grossi, our assistant archivist, we fished out the writings of our confreres during the war. Jacob Senou went through the numerous manuscripts, analysed them, and has written the article *"A glance at the Society of African Missions during World War II"*. We read the past with the experience of the present for a better future. The methodology connects the archives in Rome, the researcher in Strasbourg and the readers all over the world. The frustration of the pandemic restrictions seems insignificant when we read things like, "Unfortunately, almost all our novices are killed or missing"! If we survived that, we shall survive this pandemic!

During the same period, the magazine, *'Freres d'armes'* (Soldier Brothers) edited by the seminarians of Lyon played a vital role to connect priests and seminarians in the seminary, in missions, and at the war front. Dr. Grossi goes through the issues of the magazine during the period 1939-1945, and brings out the most prevalent themes in the writings. It is absolutely fascinating to see how priests and seminarians tried to understand their vocation, connect it to the military life and interpret their faith in the light of all that. The parallels drawn between the life of a soldier and that of a missionary, the place of Marian devotion, and the understanding of suffering are all worth pondering.

Then we move to a more recent crisis in Benin due to the ideology of Marxism and Leninism. The political change touched every aspect of the society. Michel Bonemaison who lived in Benin before, during, and after the crisis recalls how Christians and the institution of the Church were affected by the political change, and how despite everything, the Church continued to be faithful to her call at the service of humanity. Michel calls our attention to some of the present challenges with the benefit of historical hindsight.

Those who join the SMA very often say, "I was attracted by the simplicity of SMA priests". Missionary life mirrors incarnation, and finds fulfilment in self-emptying and reaching out. The entire Church continues to discover the exemplary life of the humble saint who died in the Sahara Desert - St. Charles de Foucauld. Andrea Mandonico, our archivist and postulator has also been the vice postulator for the cause of St. Charles de Foucauld. In his article *"St. Charles de Foucauld and his Missionary Vocation"*, Andrea shows how the life of de Foucauld has touched our confreres over the years. We understand better what we call the 'ministry of presence' – a valuable concept for the generation that measures everything with its immediate results.

In the article, *"Colonisation and Cultures"*, our celebrated anthropologist, Pierre Saulnier sees colonisation in the age-old framework of migration and settlement which involves power struggles, economic exploitation, and cultural confrontation. When two groups of people meet and do not share a common language, the more powerful one imposes his language to facilitate communication, and the approach is projected as promoting civilisation. Mission distinguishes itself by moving in the opposite direction through inculturation where the missionary starts by learning the culture and language of the host people as a sign of respect and appreciation. The analysis and the presentation of Pierre are quite objective, educative, and very respectful.

Vision

The *Vision* section hosts five articles. François de Paul Houngue, our Vicar General brings out a message on behalf of the General Council to the entire Society during the time of pandemic. As missionaries we realise our vocation as *guardians of the mysteries of God and guardians of each other*. Our vulnerability helps us to realise that we are creatures, and we need to be connected to God. We are also connected to each other, and therefore everybody needs to care for the good of everybody. We bear witness to this message through our missionary vocation.

Following the decision of the 2020 Plenary Council, we organised Ongoing Formation for all Unit Superiors and their Councils in September 2020 and January 2021. The September module was about 'Care for missionaries' and the January one was about 'Care for mission'. Three presentations of the September module are given in this section as articles.

James Shimbala, the Coordinator of ICOF (Inter-Congregational Ongoing Formation) Executive Committee, has been a well sought-after resource person on various topics especially the one on Resilience. The pandemic has been hammering us for over a year and we need to understand the human capacity for resilience so that we not only remain sane but also grow stronger through these trials.

While James talks of self-care in his article *"Resilience"*, François du Penhoat and Fabien Sognon, two Provincial Superiors explain the details involved in caring for members entrusted to the care of Superiors from spiritual, psychological, and administrative perspectives. Their articles show the change in leadership styles over the years and the emerging new areas where leaders need to pay more attention. Superiors exercise their leadership and brotherhood at the same time. The principles explained here are valuable for everybody since we are all guardians of each other.

In the last article of this section, *"House built for storms"*, I attempt to articulate certain disillusionment of Christians when they see day after day that pious church goers, priests, and even bishops succumb to the pandemic. The article critically looks at various interpretations of blessing, punishment, and providence, and shows how we are *empowered* and not *entitled*. The pandemic gives us an opportunity to challenge and finetune what we announce.

Spotlight

In the third section *Spotlight,* people share their experience of and their reflections on various crises in relation to mission.

Waldemar talks of the role of inculturation in mission and walks us through various challenges in the modern world and different ways of understanding inculturation. It is interesting to notice the emphasis on dialogue and meeting of cultures with genuine mutual respect without any complex since the search for truth remains the common motivation.

Ramón Bernad shares the experience of the civil war in Ivory Coast; Anthony Chukwuemeka shares the experience of floods in Nigeria; and Ephrem Kway and Paulin Kouassi share the experience of the present pandemic in the desert mission of Lodwar, and in Egypt.

Dominic Anthuvan writes about the *spiritual and mental health issues* due to and during the pandemic. As missionaries we live the same challenges as everybody else, and at the same time we also accompany and support others. The article invites us to be more mindful of what is happening, and be more resourceful so that we become more resilient, and we find ways of reaching out to the new 'most abandoned' of today.

Jonathan Malong, a formator in Ghana writes about the *Digital revolution* in the formation context. Jonathan highlights the new types of challenges we face now and invites us to be open to the advantages of the digital life and at the same time be vigilant not to compromise our essential values.

We have given the final words to the pen of a wise man – Tim Cullinane. Tim asks the question, *"Where is God in COVID-19?"*. He tries to weigh the positives and the negatives of this pandemic for the society and offers hope "Everything is going to be alright"!

I thank all those who have contributed to this bulletin. By sharing the fruit of your study and reflection, you offer a very precious service. This publication would not have been possible without the generosity of many people. I would like to name some. Brice Afferi, Dominic Wabwireh, Krzysztof Pachut, Sylvere Atta, Michel Bonemaison, and Waclaw Dominik participated in translation; Roberta Grossi offered valuable support from her expertise; and Dolores McCrystal made a major contribution for translation and proof-reading. A very important contribution to the bulletin is reading it, and making use of it. By doing these, you are reaching out to people, and you are shaping the world. That is being missionary!

S. I. Francis Rozario SMA

Our Roots

A glance at the Society of African Missions during World War II

Jacob Schiméa Senou SMA

A human story unfolds in time and space, made up of various events. For most of the time it is motorized by cogs which turn each other and thereby make the machine work. Using this image of interconnection, we can look back to re-read the story of Mission in Crisis. Any mission activity, while it is essentially *Missio Dei*, fits perfectly into human history and unfolds there. It allows itself to be affected by current events, giving people the opportunity to collaborate with the divine spirit to adapt to them. But people still need to recognize the reality of the situation they are going through and then be open to the inspiration that runs through it to them.

History will remember forever that one of the defining events of the last century was the Second World War. It was an enormous crisis of 'all humanity' which went so far as to question the whole process of humanisation - which is in fact at the heart of all evangelisation and all mission, if the latter is an authentic participation in the mission of God. We are certain about this essential element of the evangelical mission as a mission of humanisation when we remember the book of Wisdom that said of God: "By your example you taught your people that the just must be human" (Cf. Wis 12,19). As if this example which he gave were not enough, he ended up sending his incarnate Son to show people how to become "the image and likeness of God", divinisation through humanisation.

However, we are not going to retrace the history of this humanisation mission here. Having recognized that the Second World

War was a crisis which entered into it and which affected its normal course, our reflection in the following lines will consist in first setting the scene, then analysis through a review of the writings which we got from the confreres who have lived through this crisis, the challenges which were posed for them by the situation. Since human beings have a great capacity for adaptation, we will note the various responses and adaptations that they made. After this process, we could still ask ourselves how does revisiting this story help us? This is the reason for this whole exercise: we start from history so as to make us rethink the missionary responses we are giving today to the crisis caused by Covid-19.

1. Context

The Second World War does not require here an elaboration of its context of which we are all more or less aware. However, for the sake of relevance, we are referring to a time stretching from 1939-1945. This ignominy experienced by mankind plunged the whole world into an indescribable disaster the likes of which witnesses would no longer like to see repeated. The words of some of our confreres tell us that. This is the testimony left to us by Fr. Baron Pierre: "On September 16, 1943, through what anguish have I not passed! I found myself in the midst of the bombardment and I assure you that is not pleasant! [sic] ten meters from me the two vicars of the parish were killed in their presbytery. The spectacle left to us in our neighbourhood when it was over was terrible!"[1] The picture of the general condition of life, at least in certain countries of Europe, is thus painted for us through this shared experience of Pierre Baron, a member of the SMA.

During that period, the SMA had approximately 1,041 members[2] in 1939 and approximately 1,203 members[3] in 1948 (a period beyond the limit of our study). These members were on mission in at least 7 African countries (Dahomey, Egypt, Ivory Coast, Togo, Nigeria, Ghana and Liberia) with some openings beginning in the United States. It was led by Fr. Maurice Slattery, helped by Fathers [Collins], Bruhat, Hérold, Kennis, Moylan and Laubé.

---

[1] P. BARON, *Lettre au Supérieur Général*, 8 Avril 1945, AMA 11/11 B, n° 11022.
[2] Etat SMA (1939).
[3] Etat SMA (1948).

2. Challenges

The difficulties posed by the outbreak of war for the management of the Society of African Missions were of great magnitude and of all kinds. They were evident right from the centre, at the Generalate, to the missions, including formation which suffered greatly. This is also the order in which we will look at them.

2.1 Internal life and administration

The administrative system requires a cohesion which includes at least some time when the Superior General and the members of his general council can be together. However, the circumstances of the war decided otherwise for the Slattery administration. He was expected to stay in Ireland with Fr. Collins until Italy regained neutrality, in the hope of returning to Rome then. Father Bruhat was in Lyons, while Father Hérold lived in Alsace and Father Kennis was in Holland.

It is clear that this separation, which at the same time was a solution found to the difficulties, had an effect on decisions which should have been taken unanimously. The situation was probably affected by the difficulty of monitored communication during the war that we will mention later. This would undoubtedly have delayed the regrouping of all the voices necessary to reach a decision. A dispensation was therefore given by Father Slattery to his advisers to whom he wrote these words via Father Collins: "The councillor, in transmitting the decisions to be taken, will also cast his own vote so that we have a majority voice of the council. If for any urgent reason the councillor cannot wait for the response from the V. Rev. Father Superior General, he should act with the authority of the Superior General and the consent required for the case. He will then inform the V. Rev. Father Superior General"[4] of all these cases.

This desire for the decentralisation of decision-making instances was not only that of the General administration. In missions, the Ordinaries seemed to think in the same way. From Ouidah, July 14, 1944, in the name of the Ordinaries of Dahomey and Togo, meeting in Ouidah, to reflect on the urgent decisions to be taken for the sustainability of the missions during the war period, Mgr. Parisot wrote this to the Superior General: "With the permission of the Propaganda, would it not be possible to sub delegate some of your powers to Rev Fr Kennis, the

---

[4] M. SLATTERY, *Lettre au P. Bruhat*, 6 Septembre 1939, AMA 11/0 B, n° 40928.

General councillor, currently in TOGO, with the purpose of settling on the spot with the heads of Mission, all the cases that are normally the responsibility of the Provincials and the Superior General."[5]

In the light of these examples, we have some insights as to the administrative problems and how they were addressed either with stop-gap measures or more permanent solutions

2.2 Training

Formation remains an undeniably important aspect for the survival of any institution, especially an Institute of Apostolic Life or a religious Congregation. The period that we are evaluating is not one blessed with the necessary tranquillity firstly for the formation of young missionaries and also for the formation of the seminarians who were in the seminaries opened in the mission lands. The case of Dahomey will make this clear to us. However, since the flow of missionaries from this period came from the European continent, which was severely affected by the war, we will start by focusing on this.

The first element that was a challenge to missionary training was mobilisation. This expression was on everyone's lips just like that of confinement in our current crisis. In France, particularly in Strasbourg, where we have the obvious example of the Province because of its proximity to Germany, the situation was one of the least desirable. Our main witness here is Father Brediger, Provincial Superior, who deplores the conditions in which he is obliged to manage the Province. He expresses his sadness at not being able to freely make use of the buildings where his colleagues and students previously live since most of the premises were occupied: the castle of Zinswald by refugees, St Pierre by the sick and Haguenau under the weight of the military. This is not the end of his miseries. He makes a list of all the confreres who are mobilized from Haguenau, Vigneulles, Chanly and Togo and ends with this sentence which seems to give the final blow: "Our seminarians, apart from a few Poles and some Reformed, are all mobilized."[6] This sentence announces, to be precise, the near closing of a formation house. He later wrote in 1945: "Unfortunately, almost all our novices are killed

---

[5] L. PARISOT, *Lettre au Supérieur Général*, 14 Juillet 1944, AMA 12/ 802.02, n° 22809.
[6] G. BREDIGER, *Lettre au Supérieur Général*, 21 Septembre 1939, AMA 13/1, n° 12040.

or missing."[7] At that time, he had only a small remnant of his students and seminarians on whom he had to rely.

If the mobilisation of which we have just spoken touched the seminarians, it also touched the priests who were already on mission. After showing this quick picture of the situation in Alsace, let's take a historical memory tour to Benin to discover the negative impacts on formation. On November 2, 1939, from Dassa Zoumé, Bishop Parisot informed the Superior General "that out of 43 missionaries, 20 are mobilized or can be mobilized; and that it is our seminary that is the most affected by the departure of seven out of ten professors."[8] The seminary to which he refers here is undoubtedly that of Ouidah which was founded for the training of the local clergy. The numbers just referred to make it abundantly clear the extent of the difficulties experienced. However, it is clear that a difficulty that arises at the formation level has repercussions on the reduced flow of missionaries that should have come out of it.

2.3 The Mission

In reflecting on the challenges posed to missions by the humanitarian crisis, it is almost impossible to overemphasize the lack of personnel. Almost all heads of mission had experience of this. Those who did not feared it. Even at the start of the war there were not enough missionaries for the many pastoral tasks they had to perform. Unfortunately, they saw these missionary activities considerably reduced because of the mobilization of certain confreres for the war effort. The missions of the former *Francophone West Africa* (AOF) seemed to have been the most affected by this situation. Without citing them again, the statistics of Bishop Parisot in Benin have already given us a clear picture. For his part, he was obliged to teach at the seminary again to replace some of his mobilized missionaries. The case was not too different in Lomé where Bishop Cessou had already made the missionaries aware of the difficulties they would soon go through because of the absence of certain able-bodied confreres.

To this was added the fact of the travel difficulties imposed on the confreres living on the missions although they were entitled to go on vacation. The report of the Ordinaries meeting in Ouidah in 1944 allows

---

[7] IDEM, *Lettre à Bruhat*, 12 Juin 1945, AMA 13/1, n° 12274.

[8] L. PARISOT, *Lettre au Supérieur Général*, 2 Novembre 1939, AMA 12/ 802.02, n° 22791.

us to see again what was at stake for the life of the missions. Bishop Parisot wrote: "The staff in all the missions are tired. In all the French Missions, the confreres are almost everywhere alone in their stations and several Missions have already been closed due to the lack of priests. The Vicar Apostolic of Lomé urgently needs two missionaries to maintain a teacher training college of vital interest to both Togo and Dahomey."[9] The tone of this joint letter from these bishops reveals the urgency of the need in which the missions found themselves. However, the lack of staff was not the only difficulty; finances seemed to suffer as well.

The Missions in this period relied financially even more than they do today on donations arriving from Western benefactors and grants from *Propaganda Fide*. Now the war situation no longer allowed the free movement of goods. Accounts were frozen. Let's take a tour to Ireland where Fr. Stephen Harrington tells us what it was all about. On February 22, 1942, in his letter to the Superior General, he wrote: "Money transactions [...] are scrutinised very closely now when concerned with anywhere abroad [...] even for missionary purposes. In this connection I had to call the Ministry of Finance early in the New Year to make special arrangements for Liberia. Dr. Collin's account in Cork was blocked and he was not allowed to get any money whatever from Ireland."[10]

This situation was not peculiar to Ireland, but was the same in all the countries which fought against the flow of capital in order to protect their economy. Thus, Mgr. Strebler could write: "At the beginning of July 1940 the prefecture was in extreme poverty. Most of our balance was held in Europe and could not reach us, despite our best efforts. We had to take out a loan of 50,000 francs and reduce by half the already low salary of our catechists and the viaticum of our missionaries."[11] It is not necessary to dwell further on the details that paint the economic portrait of missions in that time of war. It was extremely difficult to have a flow of missionaries and money for the mission, or to get necessary information from the missions to those in leadership and vice versa.

Communication was another one of the major difficulties during the period 1939-1945. Not only was information controlled and censored from everywhere, but there was also a particular difficulty in

---

[9] IDEM, *Lettre au Supérieur Général*, 14 Juillet 1944, AMA 12/ 802.02, n° 22809.

[10] S. HARRINGTON, *Letter to Father Slattery*, 22 February 1942, AMA 14/1, n° 12848.

[11] J. STREBLER, *Rapport annuel de 1939-1940*, 14 Septembre 1940, AMA 13/ 804.07, n° 29040.

communicating with Rome. This avenue seemed totally forbidden because of the Italian political position. It is therefore obvious that such an impediment delayed decision-making. As for the missions directly, economic measures taken in some colonies had impacts on communication in the sense of the free movement of people. In Togo, where the use of vehicles using gasoline was banned for transporting people, Bishop Cessou was having difficulty continuing his pastoral visits. "As a result, in terms of 'travel' we are back 20 years ago: to the same means and slowness."[12] However, none of these missionaries remained inactive in the face of these mission conditions. Each disease has its remedy!

3. Responses and adaptations

It is important to highlight here a few points about the responses that were taken to the crisis that we have just presented. The first, which we have already mentioned above, is that of delegation with regard to crisis management in the administration and in decision-making. To avoid repeating ourselves, we simply recall that on the part of the General Council and the Heads of Mission, the first idea to compensate for the slowness of decision-making was to give each General Councillor the capacity to take urgent decisions with the necessary consultation and to notify the Superior General later. This decentralisation was not a loss of power but rather the best possible response to the difficulties associated with communication and the management of the day-to-day affairs of the Provinces and missions.

In addition, it was necessary in such circumstances to strengthen collaboration. Collaboration with obvious effect in the missions and this was what Fr. Slattery and his Council had already foreseen. He reportedly sent a circular in 1939 inviting missionaries to be willing to move from one Province to another to reinforce the confreres there. This need was communicated to him by the Ordinaries of Benin and Togo who at this time needed help. A series of investigations allow us to discover that some of these measures were taken and really served the purpose of stabilising some missions that were in difficulty in so far as they could. We take the example of the 1939-1940 report by Mgr Strebler, Apostolic Prefect of Sokodé who leaves us this testimony on the development of his missions by saying that "thanks also to the

---

[12] J. M. CESSOU, *Lettre au Cardinal Fumasoni-Biondi,* 1940, AMA 13/802.02, n° 33287, 6.

generosity of His Excellency, Monsignor Paulissen, Vicar Apostolic of Kumasi, who has kindly put at our disposal one of his best missionaries, while ours were mobilized, all our works have been maintained, and they are more prosperous than at the beginning of the war."[13] The collaboration desired and achieved between the different entities bore fruit for the sustainability of the mission. It was further supported by the training of catechists who were necessary helpers to missionaries who were exhausted despite their bravery.

This survival, however, depended not only on the presence of personnel but also on financial support. The financial crisis of the Second World War made it necessary to use the contributions of the Christian faithful to the various missions who then generously mobilized for the construction of their churches and for donations to the missions in so far as their financial situation allowed. All this required a determination to advance the mission of God with the help of the active participation of the people. It was not the idea of everybody but it appears to be one of the solutions favoured by the colleagues who lived through this crisis.

Father Aupiais, in an article entitled "The Example of the Mobilized", called this determination the *force of soul*. He notes the annihilation of individuality and identity suffered by the mobilized colleague who is only identified by a common "one"[14]. Yet, wherever they were, they knew how to put on the mantle of missionary incarnation which allowed them, despite their rank, to adapt without complaint to their situation. They learned to keep the faith through a self-effacement which can only remind us of the katabatic movement of Christ himself, praised by the hymn of Phil 2, 6-11. This spirit of sacrifice cannot help but project us into the contemporary crisis we are experiencing and which is linked to the Covid-19 virus.

In our days: Conclusion and perspectives

The aim of any historical study is to enable us to anticipate future developments while living the present in the light of past experience. Since the end of 2019, the whole world has been affected by a pandemic that it is struggling to control. For French President Emmanuel Macron,

---

[13] J. Strebler, *Rapport annuel de 1939-1940*, 14 Septembre 1940, AMA 13/ 804.07, n° 29040.
[14] Cf. F. Aupiais, "L'exemple des mobilisés", *Frères d'armes-Ralliement 2/2* (1940).

"we are at war"[15] against an invisible enemy. A war that once again plunges us into a crisis that is not fully comparable to that of World War II that we have assessed but is somewhat similar to it in terms of economic restrictions, freedom of movement and the organisation of missionary activities.

Various responses have been sought at the different organisational levels of our missions to allow us to adapt to the prevailing situation. At the very least, we are fortunate in our time to have means of communication which allow us, despite the crisis, to be connected to one another and to be able to even organize our Plenary Council and many other meetings by video conference. However, the responses provided by the older generation to the crisis they experienced could help us today to prepare for the future possibility of the decentralisation of our institutions without being unduly influenced by an overflow of 'ego' in singularity and isolation.

On the contrary, this crisis is the opportunity, as it was in the one we have just described, for a more collaborative organisation of our entities; an effort from which we have inherited the fruits through the sustainability of the mission in which the Society of African Missions participates. It allows us to understand that in our personal life there is very little that is essential and aspire to a culture where the spirit of sacrifice and resilience prevents us from constantly complaining about the difficulties we are living through.

In addition, if we have not yet understood it, we will come to understand that the reach of our mission is not only specific in a determined geographical space but now extends to innumerable people who live in a virtual space opened up to us by technological development. We are able to reach the hearts of these people without breaking the rules of the various confinements and restrictions that we live in.

Let's end with the words of this hymn that propels us into the future of the mission. *"You are the God of wide open spaces and wide horizons. You are the violent wind which pushes us forward towards the open sea, like tall ships. When you breathe in our hearts, you shake up our fears and we leave our tightly closed houses to announce you to the whole world "*.

May they be both our prayer and our invitation!

---

[15] E. MACRON, *Adresse aux Français*, 16 Mars 2020, https://www.elysee.fr/emmanuel-macron/2020/03/16/adresse-aux-francais-covid19 [consulté le 12/12/20].

"Frères d'armes" (*Soldier brothers*) 1939-1945

Roberta Grossi

A time of crisis

What is the connection between World War II and the pandemic that the world has been going through in recent months? Apparently no connection. However, one can reflect on the way in which the SMA lived and lives these moments from the point of view of "crisis".

This perspective brings us closer to Michel de Certeau's thought according to which a reading of the past is guided by a reading of the present[1] and our present is a time of crisis. From the Greek *krino*: to separate, to choose, this concept refers to arriving at clear-cut decisions. Indeed, in the field of medicine it is linked to the final outcome of a disease, the moment of hanging between life and death. In the New Testament its meaning seems to expand to encompass all decision-making situations, either in the life of the individual or in the community. During the period of Enlightenment, the term takes an additional nuance, linked to the philosophy of history. We therefore speak of history as a permanent crisis or moving beyond the temporal threshold. Both inside and outside the Christian sphere, an increasing time pressure seems to underlie everything, that is to say an advance of

---

[1] M. DE CERTEAU, *La scrittura della storia*, Jaca Book 2008, p. 30.

time, a state of uncertainty and urgency from which humanity cannot escape[2].

Finally, in the sense of rupture, the term crisis can be understood as a moment which breaks the sequence and the linearity of time. This meaning is particularly interesting in this context where we want to offer some reflections on the review *"Frères d'armes"* (Soldier brothers). It is about a bulletin written by the seminarians of Lyons from December 1909 onwards under the title *"Frères d'armes, organe mensuel du sou du soldat"* (*Soldier brothers,* source of *monthly support for soldiers*). The idea was to provide spiritual support to fellow priests and seminarians obliged to serve in the army when a French national law of 1904 abolished any type of worship in military barracks.

Fostering a common identity

From November 1939 the title changed to *"Frères d'Armes-Ralliement"* (Soldier brothers - Rally). Due to the ongoing war and the possible repercussions that this situation could have created in the usual preparation of the bulletins, the magazines of Lyons and Strasbourg were merged. In this way, the seminarians of Lyons and Rezé would try to publish at least an abridged version.

From a brief examination of the 1939-1945 war years, we note the desire to adopt an editorial line inspired by continuity. How did this idea translate into practice? What tools have been adopted? It seems clear that the basic strategy was to maintain a virtual and spiritual bond with the confreres at the frontline. This result has been achieved in various ways.

On the intellectual level the magazine offered various ideas and articles to promote reflection on theological themes as well as on missionary and political problems.

On the practical level, essential goods were sent to the front according to the specific needs of each one, thanks to the resources coming from the purchase of the bulletin by the seminarians. In the same way, the review received news including the addresses of the confreres, death notices from the front, the organisation of the chaplains and priests who were mobilized. In addition to this and not at all in contradiction, the magazine informed the readers about the progress of the missions, the news of the colleges still open and all the activities of community life that it was still possible to carry out: ceremonies, novices, priestly ordinations, work in the fields during the summer holidays, etc.

---

[2] R. KOSELLECK, *Il vocabolario della modernità*, Il Mulino 2009, pp. 95-109.

Why was it necessary to tell the story of ordinary life in this time that was nothing ordinary? The two parts had to be kept united, the two arms of the SMA then divided because of the war; a virtual bridge and information flow from both sides helped to reduce the gap and distance.

On the spiritual level, the review offered a series of prayers for confreres at war, reflections on sacred texts and on the Founder's *Retreat to Missionaries,* Jean Louis Caer (1910-1946) went even further, sending a copy of this volume to the front, where it was read and much appreciated. In this period of humiliations and contradictions, the words of the founder were an essential tool to motivating oneself in missionary life. Writing is thus transformed into a meeting place. The written text overcomes barriers and borders, it becomes the means to look to the future, to go beyond the difficulties and discouragement of the period, to build in the midst of destruction and unite in the midst of division. It fills a gap, establishes continuity and strengthens the identity of the order at this time of crisis. It was necessary to transmit the community spirit to the confreres and this was only possible through the written text which represented concrete spiritual help. There were many topics covered during these years, but some seem particularly relevant to the ability to keep the sense of identity together.

Common themes

• First of all, I would like to highlight the reflections on the Virgin, a source of consolation and spiritual support for the religious in war zones. Veneration of Mary manifests itself as an identifying trait of the missionary whose devotion seems to go further than that which other Christians have for her. Indeed, the Virgin is the guide and the help in the intellectual, moral and spiritual formation of the missionary, a support to forge the character, the one who inspires him in the learning of the rules and guides his discipline and his asceticism. In the pagan context where he works this cult acquires a greater importance since woman is not the object of respect which one notices in Christianity.

Paul Falcon (1917-1980) in the article of June 1944 *"The Star of an Apostle's Life"*, devotes a few pages to the life of the founder and his devotion to Mary who accompanied him throughout his life. The chronicle moves on two parallel tracks – on the one side some of Brésillac's meditations on the Virgin in relation to the most important stages of his missionary experience and on the other side Brésillac's message which could promote awareness among confreres to the devotion to the Mother of God. *"Let us awaken in ourselves the tender piety that we had for her from an early age [...] It is to Her, we have no doubt, that we owe the sublime vocation which commits us to walk close to Jesus"*.

- The second aspect that I want to note, recurrent in many articles, concerns the comparison of the figure of the soldier to that of the missionary whose experience takes place "outside" - beyond national borders – and linked to the ability to open oneself to the reality of the other. From this point of view, the news from Africa was essential to awaken and preserve in those who were at war the hope of the missionary role which awaited them in the future. In January 1942 the review published Gallo's article *"To your future young man from France"* in which the role of the missionary and the soldier is equated to that of a guide who organises and directs like a leader. A delicate task in preparation for which great emphasis was placed during the formation process: *"learning to go beyond ourselves, to make ourselves all for all, and to dare"*. The author did not fail to anchor his reflections in the atmosphere of the time when everyone was called to contribute to the work of national reconstruction, working to *"give back her soul to France"*.

- As a third point I would like to address what seems to me to be a dominant theme among the articles of this period, the magazine's attempt to offer practical tools to community members, for reflections and ideas to prepare them for missionary commitments. In this sense, the contributions of Francis Aupiais (1877-1945) can be considered as actual teaching on ministry. The article *"Unum Ovile"* (September-October 1941) developed various aspects which clearly expressed the idea of vocation and apostolic life that the two "separate branches" of the SMA were to continue to pursue together. Exercises and spiritual retreat, reading of the Constitutions in the refectory, prayer for the conversion of Africa were, for the author, the elements necessary to maintain the sense of unity which should always be present among confreres. *"To be united in the same vocation by the same oath, for the same apostolic ends [...] however, the separated sheep must not be dispersed, which means that they must not lose the invisible bonds which hold them together and will continue to hold them together better than all visible presences"*.

In his essay of March 1942 Aupiais examines the ideas of Pius XI, relating to the African people, which were expressed during the meeting of 1928: *"When you return to your Africans, you will tell them that I love them for what they are"*. To love the African people not out of pity and charity but for their spiritual wealth and good faith represents for Aupiais a far-sighted apostolic action program that every missionary should never forget. In December 1942 he recalls the apostolic work of François Steinmetz (1868-1952) on the occasion of the fiftieth anniversary celebrated in Whydah. Above all, the missionary is admired for the example he gives regarding being in harmony with the African populations and demonstrating how to *"adapt, bring closer, universalize"*. Aupiais also emphasized his diplomatic competence thanks to which he could often be well received by the indigenous authorities, even obtaining recognition of his role and authority. Far from marginal, respect for traditions and the learning of the local language was important to Steinmetz who *"learned Dahomean (Fon), to become Dahomean among Dahomeans"*.

Addressing themes far removed from the problem of war and its consequences proved to be a skilful strategy for the magazine, which could thus convey messages of comfort and support. Transmitting news of daily life, exams, studies, community activities, was intended to keep alive, among confreres at the front, the hope of one day being able to regain total "normality". At a deeper level, the essays on more complex themes would have made it possible to pursue a kind of "distance learning" so as not to completely interrupt the link of the young people with their formation, at the same time fuelling the spirit of knowledge and the desire to be a missionary.

• The last point I would like to consider answers the question concerning the journal's attitude in regard to the war. I have already underlined the sections on the reports from the front, the imprisonment of confreres and on the SMA houses occupied or affected by the bombardments and destruction. But what I would especially like to clarify is that it is, however, "writing in a time of crisis" and that the theme of suffering imbues all the issues of the magazine and is addressed in various ways. The meaning of the drama of this period is well expressed in the April 1943 article by Father Joseph Delhommel (1885-1978), *"Redemptive Suffering"*. Here the author approaches the theme of the theology of suffering from the entry *"Church"* of Father Médiebelle of the Sacred Heart of Betharran of Nazareth, in the *Dictionary of the Bible*. *"To suffer is to complete Christ, it is to extend him, to replace him, for the same redemptive ends and in the same way [...] Like Paul, every Christian also has a vocation, through his sufferings, to complete Jesus*

Christ"[3]. Suffering is educative and for Christians it is enlightened by faith; it is faith that enables him to become aware of the reason for suffering, *"Man is an apprentice, pain is his master"*. It conforms us to Jesus Christ and the Cross is the sign of our alliance, of our collaboration with him. I believe that in these lines there is an abbreviated indicator of the spirit of the time.

Today - Restoring unity to humanity

Finally, let's return to the word crisis and its connection to the current Covid pandemic by specifying that the search for familiarity with the past, although reassuring, does not help to understand emergencies and the problems of the present. Today's Covid is something other than the plague of yesterday. However, we can reflect on the Pope's declaration *"No one saves himself alone"* which seems to me particularly true regarding the work of the missionary. He crosses the whole world to reconnect the pieces of humanity, reaffirming everywhere the validity of his ministry, so he already has mastery of the tools and the necessary means to translate into reality the call of the Pope. It seems that the review *Frères d'Armes* was moving in these directions when it sought to promote and foster the unity of a community separated and torn apart by the events of war.

---

[3] A. MÉDEBIELLE, *Church, mystical body of Christ*, in L. PIROT (ed.), *Dictionary of the Bible containing all the names of people, places, plants, animals mentioned in the Holy Scriptures, theological, archaeological, scientific questions, critiques relating to the Old and New Testaments and notes on ancient and modern commentators.* Supplement II, Letouzey and Ané, 1934, col. 666.

Marxism-Leninism in Dahomey-Benin: a Challenge for the Christian Faith

Michel Bonemaison SMA

History: conscience and clairvoyance

In this article I do not claim to present a comprehensive analysis of the period of Marxism-Leninism that we lived through in Dahomey- Benin from 1974 onwards, nor dwell on one of the different phases that we underwent. I only propose to revisit, from my own perspective, a few facts of life which could, in these sensitive and difficult times, attract attention, challenge reflection, and stimulate individual or joint action.

1.   A meeting of young priests in 1969

As early as 1965, when I was a teacher at the minor seminary of Parakou, in Dahomey, my contact with the French youth coming to help in public high schools, as part of the 'teaching collaboration programme' allowed me to spot the Marxist[1] ideology that some brought in their suitcases in the "service of young Dahomeans" and… of the Nation.

During a meeting of "young priests", shortly after Easter 1969, we talked of the impact of such a philosophy and wondered if one could measure the spread of "atheism" among the young people, particularly students; we even suggested that an ongoing formation in this area could be helpful to chaplaincies!

---

[1] The periods of compulsory military service 1961-1963 allowed me to appreciate the influences at work among many of my colleagues.

2. A slogan: "We have chosen, we no longer have a choice"

Back from vacation in September or October 1974, in Malanville I quietly cross the bridge over the Niger and, once the customs operations have been cleared, I see a huge and magnificent billboard; a novelty! On it is announced a whole political program summarized in its slogans:

Socialism is our guide.

Marxism-Leninism is our way.

We have chosen, we no longer have a choice.

I was going to say "Listen whoever can hear!" - *"qui potest capere capiat!"* It is in the bag. History would bear this out during the next seventeen years of dictatorship.

3. Attacks on human freedom

It seems that the aim is to "do a *tabula rasa*" of all the past and in particular of the recent history which bears the name of "colonialism". Foreigners out, thus are targeted all those who represent a recent section of the history of conquest through arms and for the sake of trade: "Colonialism - Down with it!", "Neo-colonialism - Down with it! »

God does not exist, therefore the expulsion of Catholic and Protestant religious have begun, not Muslims of course because they are already part of the landscape, even if some populations have only recently arrived on the soil of the current People's Republic: "The religious – Down with it!"," The neo-religious - Down with it!"

Through education we must take all youth in hand and protect them from the harmful influences of Western philosophies, because Marxism comes from a Higher plane than the Enlightenment, no doubt: "the occult - Down with it!", "Neo-obscurantism, Down with it!" I must say that the effort of this period bore undeniable fruit because the coercion is so intense that the percentage of children going to school is enormous. Unfortunately, the teachers are ideologically trained and so are the children in the school for the good of the nation. But the movement will be irreversible, and the teaching will flourish. *"Alea jacta est!*[2]*"*

Let us come back to school, a place where we educate people, particularly in the civic sense. But here we obviously have to deal with the destruction of the family or the social environment, the denial of

---

[2] "The die has been cast"

parental authority, etc. This is how children learn to denounce (without malice on their part, which calls into question the formation of conscience) the attitude of adults in their environment. Learning utter denunciation! The result? How many parents are arrested by the police, at night as is fitting, and placed in pre-trial detention which soon turns into total disappearance. Look no further, they have been declared harmful to the Republic. The game is up.

We could continue the litany inviting everyone to shout " Down with it!" with their left fist raised, without forgetting neo-colonialism, neo-liberalism, neo-regionalism and all the possible and unimaginable neos; the best one is the result of the sense of humour of our President himself; some took it as a slip of the tongue and made fun of him, but he knows very well the race for power and the nepotism that has always plagued governments in Africa, (to speak only of our continent), through kinship, political parties, regional influences etc. So at the end of a speech to complete the litany of things " Down with it!", inventing his own word for the abuse of power to be denounced he exclaims: "Neopotism" and all answer raising their left fists: "Down with it!" Are we already living a happy Utopia?

When one is surrounded by the pernicious lies, the aberrations of one of these indefinable ideologies used by the Evil One, how can the disciples of Christ conduct themselves? Take note, reflect, pray, act with prudence and count on the community dimension i.e. the ecclesial?

The Church: Christians and her ministers

These are still only small flashes of truly personal experience.

1. In Bembérékè, 1969-1976

An anachronistic presidential attitude. The last tour of the President-in-Office seems to be aimed at securing the support of all the military forces of the Nation because shortly after his visit each of us, in all the missions of the North-East receive a visit from the commander of the gendarmerie and the commander of the military camp, who come privately, each in turn, to assure us of the unwavering protection of the national security forces.

Then on the way back, the President and his wife stop at the house for a courtesy visit and a moment of fraternal friendship around "a good cold beer". But he also summons the Sub-Prefect who, in front of me, is reprimanded which amazes me! Immediately "two students" of the sub-prefecture Marc studying medicine and Roger history are brought there by soldiers. After their departure I allow myself to express, to our Friend, how much I am dismayed by his anachronistic remarks to the rising generation and I reveal to him my bitterness with regard to the unjust sanctions he inflicts on them. Madame agrees with this saying: "Listen to what the Father says".

Marc goes into exile in Togo to pursue his medical studies in peace. Roger will not go to France for his doctorate. A few weeks later the government falls. There was already something going on! Roger becomes one of the prominent figures of the new power base which, shortly after, switches to Marxism-Leninism to free the country from a certain number of political archaisms. Fortunately, we keep excellent relations with Marc and Roger.

Denouncing. The new regime settles down openly endorsing the dictatorship, the lies, the culture of hatred, and obviously of denunciation. Often, among colleagues, we discuss the anti-educational influence that these elements can have on children and young people. And I myself try in vain to draw attention to one element, oh how harmful! the denunciation which so distorts the young consciences. Several cases of disappearance of mum or dad torn from their young children have been reported to me following innocent words: nocturnal arrest, and pure and simple disappearance. Some colleagues tell me that I will be in trouble, I would like them to be right.

The homilies. Imagine that we are being watched, we priests! spied on, we expatriates! Everyone reacts in his own way, according to his temperament. But we have to be very careful. One of us was simply confiding in a friend who provided a wonderful social service in the field of health. (it was too burdensome for this friend who, one day unwittingly, betrayed him!) Another colleague, most meticulous, wrote each of his homilies word for word and never strayed from it one iota (there are iotas also in French!). As for me, knowing that I was being watched, I gave my opinion and gave advice only in the local language, or with great courtesy. Thus, one day after the homily, a gentleman, our postman, came to find me and said: "Really if I denounce you for what you have just said, I will be taken for an imbecile" and I retort "Denounce me quickly, because the other spy has already reported my preaching in high places, do not be outdone". The Gospel of the day had just given me the opportunity to thank the Revolution for inviting former Christians to come back to the Church, mandating them to listen and pass on our words through detailed reports.

Literacy. One of our means of approaching the people is an unprecedented service in Borgou: since colonisation, the education of children seems to have come up against an uncooperative environment; the mission has hardly been any more successful. On the other hand, adult literacy in the local language immediately arouses a lot of interest to such an extent that the Marxist Revolution forbids us to be involved in it because it is extensive enough to take over, which it does very well.

All over the country, the Church is robbed of all its primary schools and most of its colleges. In the North, we still have adult literacy. The Revolution is keenly aware of its importance, thinking that it is still an area of great influence, human, even spiritual. It takes ownership of it! But it acts without thinking about the reaction of the facilitators-trainers who, almost every day, very discretely continue to come and study their lessons with us, the original teachers. Appearances are preserved, instruction and education take their course.

What reading can be offered to a people who are beginning to know how to read and write, and who love this new means of communication? Thanks to the know-how of the National Linguistics Commission, the new literates can read a monthly called "kparo - the Herald". Also, eager to read, many are now reading daily the Word of God that is available through the New Testament by Father Leonard or through the Bible of the Evangelical Church. We take this opportunity to distribute in our communities comments on the liturgical texts for each Sunday. The photocopiers are running wild in each parish! Evangelisation takes on a new face. Thanks be to God and to the Marxist-Leninist Revolution.

2. In Bagou in association with Joseph my neighbour 1976-1979

Joseph is my closest colleague; he directs the diocesan training centre for catechists located in the parish of Bagou of which I am the pastor. Our fraternal life consists essentially of a critical and regular pooling of our perception of daily reality. Jo shows great insight, and he collects the seemingly insignificant little details which, taken together, highlight the whole prevalent ideology.

The election of mayors. To better organize the territory, the government thinks it has to break the authority of the traditional chiefdom and create new administrative structures to "hand over power to the people". Thus each community must elect its delegate and each municipality (newly established) will elect its mayor. The ideological training meetings are not very convincing and people do not understand much about these elections that have come out of a feudal mould.

We should move from feudalism to democracy, this is the project hammered into all the speeches and by all the restructuring of the People's Commissar. So who are the people to turn to in order to understand what has just been so often repeated? Here I am, a social advisor, but acting with the utmost discretion. With me always available in my room-office-kitchen, the others waiting in the courtyard as if for confession, I reflect on the qualities that those to be elected in the future must have. In the end all the delegates and most of the mayors are from the feudal oligarchy, Muslims or pagans (there is not yet a Christian community in this sector).

The people will be well guided and I will be kept minutely informed of all the advances of the Revolution. A quote from a speech by the People's Commissar was humorously reported to me: "Beware of the priest, he knows Marxism better than you and I. Go visit his library and you will understand".

Joseph and I will still have to leave our parishes, but we escape the expulsion that has been the fate of many religious expatriates. Our bishop, an African, does not allow himself to be intimidated and goes to the Presidency where, after much humiliation, he gets a promise that no more religious will be expelled.

3. In Wenu 1980-1983

After a time of retreat, I gladly welcome my bishop's proposal to come as pastor to Wenu-Kpakeru. Like all my colleagues I am really limited in my travels to visit the villages scattered over more than 2000 km². The people are most welcoming, but I have to be careful. The "comrade district chief" (sub-prefect) does not hesitate to remind me of the restrictions imposed by the regime. How can we meet the challenge and continue to visit those whom the Lord has entrusted to us and who, frustrated by the limits imposed by ideology, perceive a plan of salvation that listens to the eternal newness that is the Gospel?

A Godsend occurs: the Director of the state college which opens is alongside the parish territory has only two professors; N'Dali, although a commercial crossroads, is still a small village little coveted as a place of work by officials. Here I am an employee of the academy as a French teacher in the service of a class of 120 sixth graders (40 x 3). My bishop agrees that I should take up such a role with the young people: considered their dean by the directors of small village schools, I am invited to visit each of their establishments; I take this opportunity to get closer to the parishioners. Everyone's honour is saved! I know that in the country others have been given such commitments, for example John to teach philosophy.

Forty years later, we find several of these young people in positions of responsibility in various civic and ecclesial bodies in the country.

4. Rome to Cotonou on February 17, 1982.

Cardinal Gantin invites John Paul II to visit Cotonou, a prophetic step! From Wenu-Kpakeru, my new parish, 16 of us go in a 504 van to meet the Holy Father. Only Saria, elder sister of Father Jacques, and her nephew Pierre are baptized. He is invited to read a section of the Universal Prayer at the Pontifical Mass and his aunt receives communion from the hand of Pope John Paul. All come back with the words of our "Father" in the depths of their hearts:

"Evangelisation must also enlighten, purify and uplift all the customs and traditions which so strongly permeate the souls of your compatriots, in order to absorb all that can contribute to a life more in conformity with the Christian faith and, ultimately, more deeply human. Consciences must be carefully helped in this discernment: thus, freed from fear, the faithful can progress in peace, developing the best of themselves, with the cultural riches that they can and must keep, but in accepting the demands and, if necessary, the sacrifices imposed by the Gospel. Thus Christians will be truly worthy of Christ, keeping the vigour of salt or leaven in the dough, and their faith will not fade away in the ambiguity of dangerous syncretism.[3]»

On our return we stop at the Marian grotto of Dassa to entrust the conversion of our country to the Lord through the intercession of the one who said « Yes » to the depths of her womb. The face of our parish begins to change, the whole country emerges "strengthened" from this pastoral visit, around an immense Eucharistic Assembly experienced at the Akpakpa stadium.

5. Monsignor Isidore de Souza and the nation

A short time later and it is the Archbishop of Cotonou, Monsignor Isidore de Souza, who is appointed to guide the country in this return to democracy. He chairs the National Conference from February 19 to 28, 1990. He continues to support the country until the presidential

---

[3] Apostolic pilgrimage to Nigeria, Benin, Gabon and Equatorial Guinea, Mass, Homily of John Paul II, Cotonou (Benin), Wednesday, February 17, 1982.

elections. The country is emerging from its politico-ideological monolithism, but it must make a real assessment of the shortcomings and hopes at stake. It has been thirty years! What assessment, what future?

What challenges for us today?

Today, after thirty years of democracy, are there any challenges that the Church must tackle, in herself, in the life of the Nation, in connection with the planet? Are we able to discern the warning signs of the crises which are coming towards us just as they have affected humanity elsewhere? Beyond the name, which limits us locally to Benin, this interrogation is meant to bring to the surface questions for other local churches.

To be faithful to her mission, the Church, wherever it is, cannot rest on its laurels and so it must embark on the path of reflection, constantly highlighting the value of hard work. Locally, it must become aware of the shortcomings that the Universal Church faces today and in the contemporary world: either omnipotent materialism or boundless liberalism and, as concerns itself, the scandals about money and dubious behaviour which all crystallize in a lack of respect for the human person. Nothing should be allowed to slip through the cracks!

1. In the schools and chaplaincies

Courageously resuming its place in society, the Church in Benin resolutely works for the good of the population at the level of the intellectual development of the people by opening a large number of schools in villages and neighbourhoods and developing colleges, and even Catholic faculties. But what education can it offer while ensuring harmony with the teachings according to the government standards? To whom are the chaplaincies of public establishments entrusted and what religious, moral and social training is offered to both the laity and religious in charge of education?

Also, regarding the content of the training to be given, Pope Francis reminds us *"that God desires the happiness of his children, on earth too, although they are called to eternal fullness, since he created all things. "so that we may enjoy it"* so that all may enjoy it. It follows that Christian conversion requires a special reconsideration of all that concerns the social order and the *achievement of the common good"* [4]. This is a first challenge for the quality of education within the Nation.

2. Both public and private health service

Under the Marxist-Leninist regime Christian health workers were very courageous; by organizing themselves they were able to avoid the nationalisation of everything that the churches, both Catholic and those resulting from the Reformation, had already implemented. The demography is growing and the various churches can continue for a long time to maintain such social work in partnership with the State.

But in the contemporary world selfish ideas erode respect for life and for old age, endanger the truth of God's presence in human life at home and in hospital. and risk destroying the family. This today is a heart-breaking reality in the West. Will we be able to discern in time the warning signs of this challenge for the Gospel in Africa? In my opinion a lot depends first and foremost on the family which can be an antidote to selfishness, and a place of strength for real action in today's world. Let us simply reread *"Amoris Laetitia"* the apostolic exhortation of Pope Francis on Love in the family or "The Joy of the gospel" 2016.

3. Shortcoming of the Church and dishonesty of ministers

Our defects are many; let us be vigilant with regard to lukewarmness and carelessness which "prowl like lions looking for someone to devour"; by developing our emotional maturity, let us prevent scandals from ravaging our ecclesial family; secondly, abuse of power through access to money within communities is not an illusion but a reality and can lead to nepotism or a double life. Are we ready to meet or even anticipate these challenges?

A renewed pastoral formation (which is carried out in many places thanks in particular to the parents in the families) at the seminary and for pastoral workers could make us better aware of the setbacks due to these defects which constantly threaten us within the Church and its ministers.

The Pandemic with its many episodes shows us that the diabolical race for selfish comfort is still persistent today even if many in the world are slowly experiencing a real conversion to "respect for the human

---

[4] POPE FRANCIS, Apostolic Exhortation *Evangelii Gaudium*, (24 November 2013), 4/I, 182

person" and a solid return to the "sense of the Common Good". What can we do in our local Church? It is a real challenge for today, and it is once again Pope Francis, herald of the Good News, who by his interpretation of current events, enlightened by the values of the Gospel, knows how to guide us towards a true conversion for the greater glory of the Lord. Let us read and meditate on his encyclical *"Laudato Si'"*, "Praise be to you[5]" to discern how we can live today.

---

[5] POPE FRANCIS, Encyclical Letter *Laudato Si'* (24 May 2015), 1.

St. Charles de Foucauld and his Missionary Vocation

Andrea Mandonico SMA

An important aspect linked to the canonisation of Charles de Foucauld - of whom I am the vice-postulator - is his priestly ministry among Muslims. It is my deep conviction, despite being a fairly widespread idea, that Bro. Charles[1] did not go into the desert to live "as a hermit",

---

[1] Charles-Eugene de Foucauld, Viscount of Pontbriand, was born on September 15, 1858 in Strasbourg (France). Having lost both his father and mother at the age of 6, he was entrusted to his maternal grandfather who raised him like "a little prince". While in high school, he lost his faith. Like all the nobles of his time, he chose a military career in St Cyr, then in Saumur, living a dissipated lifestyle, except for the year when he explored Morocco (1883-1884).

Returning to Paris at the end of October 1886, he converted. During a pilgrimage to the Holy Land, he discovers the mystery of Jesus living in Nazareth: he feels called to imitate him throughout his life. In search of this imitation he will enter the order of Trappists (1890-1897), after which he will go as a servant to the Poor Clares of Nazareth (1897-1900).

He returned to France where on June 9, 1901 he was ordained a priest for the diocese of Viviers (Ardèche). He will go to live in the Sahara, in Beni-Abbés and afterwards in Tamanrasset. On December 1, 1916 he was killed by Senoussite looters.

On November 13, 2005, the Church declared him Blessed and, on May 26, 2020, Pope Francis signed the decree which recognizes the second miracle and therefore his canonization.

seeking the *fuga mundi* so dear to the first monks[2], but actually went there to evangelize and dedicate his whole life to these poorest brothers "who lack everything because they lack Jesus"[3]. He himself wrote to Father Huvelin:

"For some time now and this is increasing every day, my thoughts cannot be detached from Morocco, from its ten million inhabitants, all infidels, from this people so considerable entirely abandoned: neither a priest nor a missionary. [...] Inside, in this country as big as France, not an altar, nor a priest, nor a religious; Christmas night will be spent there without a mass, without a mouth and a heart pronouncing the name of Jesus; [...] This thought does not leave me ... "[4]

If the Church offers him to us as a model of holiness - and Pope Francis quotes him in almost all of his documents and in a particular way when he speaks not only to bishops, priests, religious but also to catechists and young people – then what does he have to teach us SMA missionaries for the third millennium?

When I am called to speak about him or to hold a conference on him or on an aspect of his life and mission, at the end there is always one person or other who comes forward to declare that he has been an important figure in his formation for the priestly or consecrated life. I also believe that among us SMA, many were seduced by this "very

---

Charles de Foucauld wanted to occupy the very least place in society and to be forgotten by everyone; he wanted to pass through this world in silence "like a traveller in the night" that no one sees and notices! But his evangelical testimony was so luminous that the Church today offers him to us as a model in his imitation and 'following' of Jesus.

[2] Cf. A. MANDONICO, "Charles de Foucauld: il volto di Cristo nel deserto", in Istituto internazionale di ricerca sul volto di Cristo (ed.), *Il volto dei volti di Cristo*, Ed. Velar 2002, vol. XVI, 181-191.

[3] This is evidenced by the letter of March 7, 1902 to his friend Gabriel Tourdes and that to Bishop Caron of April 8, 1905, or that of November 22, 1907 to Father Huvelin, his spiritual director. What is difficult, in my opinion, is not his intention but the need to find the place of Nazareth in pastoral care. So, for years, he called himself "monk", "missionary", "isolated missionary", "monk-missionary". He wrote it to Father Antonin, a Trappist, on May 13, 1911; to H. de Castries on August 14, 1901; to its Prefect Apostolic, Mgr Guérin, on June 10, 1903 and again on July 2, 1907; to his cousin, Mme de Bondy, on September 16, 1905; without forgetting the letter to Mgr Bonnet, bishop of Viviers, May 28, 1904.

[4] CDF (Charles de Foucauld), Huvelin, 205.

powerful figure of Christian spirituality"[5] during the years of our formation.

Charles de Foucauld in the life of the SMA

Working in our archives here in Rome, I have found writings which show us how Charles de Foucauld did not go unnoticed among us. On the contrary, even if we did not imitate him in full, he influenced our method of evangelizing and interacting with Africans and their culture. I will cite only a few examples.

a)   Shortly after his death (1916) his influence on the missionaries became more and more important. In the preface to the book Deux sœurs noires[6] the abbot of La Trappe, Father Chautard, while writing a letter to Father Aupiais, said that he had had "an interview with Father de Foucauld, who in our order prepared himself for his sublime vocation in Africa"[7]. He then invited the sisters to live "a strongly mixed life, where contemplation at least equals action". It was the style of "the life of Nazareth" of Bro. Charles de Foucauld[8] that Fr. Aupiais, in his long introduction, would promote and recommend to the sisters.

b)   For the centenary of his birth, the *Echo des Missions Africaines de Lyon* (n. 5 - 1958) presents him to colleagues as a "Great African Figure; Great Missionary figure". Fr. Urvoy, after having outlined the chronology of his life, leaves the floor to Fr. Aimé Roche, OMI, to recount his life and label him as the great missionary who "will soon break forth across the five continents in an astonishing germination… ". The long article ends with a few sentences from Charles de Foucauld himself. I will only quote this one which seems to me very close to the apostolate of our first confreres who went to the extent of giving their lives: "Let us love all men as Jesus loved them, wishing as much good for them as He wished for them, doing all the good in our power for them, devoting ourselves to their salvation, ready to give our blood for the salvation of each of them".

c)   The Province of Italy in 2002 held a day of recollection during its "mini-assembly" on the spirituality of Bro. Charles and I believe that many of us recognized ourselves in it.

---

[5] P. MARTINELLI, *Vite meravigliose*, Ed. Terra Santa 2018, 115.

[6] RELIGIEUSE DE LA SAINTE-FAMILLE DU SACRÉ CŒUR, *Deux sœurs noires*, Ed. Librerie Bloud & Gay 1931.

[7] IDEM, 7.

[8] IDEM, 17.

d) In addition, a few years ago I preached a recollection to our confreres in Montferrier on evangelisation according to Charles de Foucauld. Many of them thanked me for having given them the opportunity to be missionaries even in a nursing home through their Eucharistic celebration, their holiness, prayer,[9] etc.

---

[9] In *Article XXVIII* of the Directory which he writes for his future disciples, he lists the *"General means and particulars for the conversion of souls distant from Jesus, and especially infidels. -* For the conversion of souls and especially for that of infidels, the brothers and sisters will employ above all the following ten means:
1 ° the Holy Sacrifice of the Mass, by increasing the number of Masses celebrated among the infidels, by having Masses applied for their conversion, and praying devoutly for this conversion during the Holy Sacrifice;
2 ° the Most Blessed Sacrament, by increasing the number of Tabernacles among infidels, by developing the cult of the Blessed Eucharist in non-Christian countries, and by praying devoutly before the Blessed Sacrament for the conversion of infidels;
3 ° personal sanctification, for the soul does good in accordance with its own holiness;
4 ° prayer;
5 ° penance, that is to say sacrifice, acceptance of crosses sent by God and acts of voluntary mortification authorized by the spiritual director;
6 ° good example, by being models of evangelical life, by showing the Gospel in their life, by being living Gospels, such that by seeing them one knows what Christian life is, what the Gospel, what Jesus is;
7 ° goodness, to make themselves loved and to make people love all that is about them, their religion and Jesus their Master;
8 ° the establishment of friendly relations with people, with constant care to do good to their souls, going to those one wants to convert and particularly to infidels, mingling with them and becoming close friends with them;
9 ° the help given to priests, men and women religious who work for the salvation of souls in the place where one is, and particularly to those who work there for the conversion of infidels;
10 ° the help given to priests, men and women religious who work for the salvation of souls outside the place where one is, and particularly to those who work for the conversion of infidels", C. DE FOUCAULD, *Règlements et Directoire (Tome XI et XII de l'édition intégrale)*: (de 1896 jusqu'en 1916), M. BOUVIER (ed.), Nouvelle Cité 1995, 591-592.

Cardinal Tisserant on the method of Charles de Foucauld

I found in the archives a long letter from Card. Tisserant, then Prefect of the Sacred Congregation "Pro Ecclesia Orientali", from 27.04.1939, to our Superior General, Fr. Maurice Slattery[10].

In this long letter (4 pages), the Cardinal asks Fr. Slattery to prepare missionaries ready to go to the world of Muslims to convert them, because it seems that the time is appropriate. To support his request, the Cardinal quotes the letter of 25.03.1225 from Pope Onorio III in which he asked the abbots of Citeaux, Cluny, Clairveaux, Saint Colombano for religious for this apostolate[11]. The Cardinal is convinced that despite the times being changed, the call to ministry among Muslims still remains valid. Certainly there are still many difficulties, but now we know more about the people, their ways and customs, "Islamic things", helped in this by colonisation. But he also knows that "the preparation of missionaries for the conversion of Muslims is a very delicate task, because of the violent reactions that can easily arise due to the smallest of mistakes that the missionaries despite their best intentions can make; very zealous but not very enlightened".

To cater for this, the cardinal asks our Superior General to open "a college or a school [...] in Muslim territory, with a name similar to that of the *"Institut des Belles-Lettres Arabes"* of Tunis"[12]. He is convinced that "this college or school would give missionaries destined to work among Muslim populations the very careful and specialized formation which is absolutely required for such an apostolate and which cannot be delivered in other houses of study or training". He concludes writing: "If your religious congregation cannot or does not consider it the opportune moment to found a college or a school of this kind, it can send the fathers to be prepared for the apostolate among the Muslims to one of the already existing institutes or one about to be founded in the regions closest to those where your missionary congregation works ".

---

[10] Cf. E. G. G. Tisserant, *Lettre au Supérieur Géneral*, 1939, AMA 11/8.03.07 n. 27049.

[11] The Cardinal, following the example of Pope Onorio III°, addresses the religious because "by living under a rule and leading a life oriented to perfection, they are the most able to travel the world and preach the Gospel there *'verbo et exemplo'"*.

[12] Today PISAI with its headquarters in Rome, still entrusted to the White Fathers.

Then he exhorts: "This Dicastery, in perfect agreement with the Sacred Congregation of P [ropaganda] F [ide], maintains that each mission which has a large number of Muslims, should have one or more missionaries dedicated to this very delicate task which is to be undertaken with all the necessary precautions and according to the method established by the most highly authorized directives ".

What is this method?

Cardinal Tisserant[13] offers some typically Foucauldian methodological guidelines.

1. *"The moment seems to have arrived [...] to begin a process of coming closer and understanding intended to break down the prejudices of Muslims and to put [...] their souls in contact with the spiritual values of Christianity".*

It is impossible not to think of Bro. Charles when he affirmed that his work in the Sahara was to prepare the ground for the missionaries who would come after him. On April 3, 1906 he wrote to Father Caron:

"My work here is only a work of preparation, of first clearing: it is first of all to place amongst them Jesus, Jesus in the Most Holy Sacrament, Jesus becoming present every day in the holy Sacrifice: it is to put in their midst a prayer, the prayer of the Holy Church"[14].

On July 29, responding to R. Bazin, his future biographer, who asked him for information on Catholic missions in Algeria, Charles de Foucauld reminded him of his pastoral method:

"Isolated missionaries like me are very rare; their role is to prepare the way, so that the missions which will replace them find a friendly and trusting population, souls to some degree prepared for Christianity, and, if possible, a few Christians "[15]

This silent preparation in order to welcome Jesus is done by "good example", that is to say, according to what he wrote in the Directory for his brothers, always seeking to be "models of evangelical life, by making them see the Gospel in their life, by being living Gospels, so that by

---

[13] Some will wonder how Cardinal Tisserant knew CDF so well. He was the Cardinal protector of the Little Sisters of Jesus and undoubtedly the foundress, ps Madeleine de Jésus, had transmitted this knowledge to him.

[14] C. DE FOUCAULD, *XXV Letters to Abbé Caron*, 20.

[15] R. BAZIN, *Charles de Foucauld explorateur du Maroc*, Ermite au Sahara, Plon 1923, 442.

seeing them we know what Christian life is, what the Gospel is, what Jesus is "[16].

It is not a good moral example but rather a good Christological example: "To be a model of evangelical life, that is to say of Jesus" because "the priest is a monstrance, his role is to show JESUS; he must disappear and show JESUS "[17]. Immediately afterwards, so as not to have us remain in the dark, he adds: "To strive to leave a good memory in the soul of all those who come to me"[18].

2. *"To preach to them, openly about the Trinity, the Incarnation, the Sacraments, in certain places could constitute the most serious recklessness and could compromise centuries of hope".*

Bro Charles, on March 6, 1908, wrote to his Prefect Apostolic: "I do not believe that Jesus wants either me or anyone to preach Jesus to the Tuaregs. This would be the way to delay, not to advance, their conversion. It would lead them to distrust us, to move away rather than bringing them closer"[19].

He is well aware that this method can last a long time, but no matter: "It is a long-term work, requiring dedication, virtue and constancy. […] This being done, the conversions at the end of a variable time, twenty-five years, fifty years, a hundred years, will come by themselves, just as the fruits ripen"[20].

3. *"The method of 'becoming familiar', as Charles de Foucauld said, must be well studied, not only in connection with Islam in general but also with regards to the local cultural differences."*

For his part Charles de Foucauld declared:

"We must become accepted by the Muslims, become for them the dependable friend, to whom one goes when in doubt or in pain; on whose affection, wisdom and righteousness one relies absolutely. It is only when we have got to this point that we can succeed in doing good to their souls. My life therefore consists of being as close as possible to what surrounds me and of rendering all the services that I can"[21].

A friendship that is not imposed, but is offered; go to them, be always available to the neighbour but also to all those who knock on the

---

[16] ivi, note 9.

[17] C. DE FOUCAULD, *Carnets de Tamanrasset*, 188.

[18] IBIDEM.

[19] C. DE FOUCAULD, *Correspondances sahariennes*, 605-606.

[20] R. BAZIN, *Charles de Foucauld*, 409.

[21] IDEM, 443.

door, sharing their life; he will pray for them; he will become the reliable friend and advisor sought after for his wisdom and his sense of justice.

4. *"We have often proclaimed as an ideal, comprehensive and effective formula, this maxim" Charity and prayer".*

a) Charity

Fr Charles left an ideal mission to his heirs: "It is the mission of the little brothers of the Sacred Heart of Jesus, in accordance with their name, to make JESUS and CHARITY reign. They must make JESUS and CHARITY reign, in their hearts and around them"[22]. They "do not save by preaching [...] but they save by charity, charity of seeing in every human being nothing but a member of the body of Jesus to be filled with goods and to lead to heaven, the immense and universal charity which must radiate fraternity"[23].

Charity which, in his writing, also goes by the name of goodness. Returning from a trip to France in 1909, Bro. Charles wrote in his diary the advice received from Father Huvelin, his Spiritual Director:

"My apostolate must be the apostolate of goodness. Seeing me one must say to oneself: "Since this man is so good, his religion must be good." "- If you ask why I am gentle and good, I must say:" Because I am the servant of someone who is much better than I am. If you only knew how good my Master JESUS is"[24].

Goodness which is not only the performance of good deeds but becomes a style of life, a dimension of our whole life and not only a fragment of our time or our action.

b) Prayer

Bro. Charles felt called to imitate Jesus in His life in Nazareth, where Jesus had lived for 30 years. He was, however, Saviour in a hidden way, that is to say not visible to human eyes, but truly effective and divine: prayer has an apostolic fruitfulness and is a true form of apostolate, a true apostolate. He wrote to Louis Massignon:

"Think a lot about others, pray a lot for others. To devote yourself to the salvation of your neighbour through the means in your power, prayer, kindness, example, etc ... it is the best way to prove to the divine Spouse that you love him: "Whatever you do to one of these little ones,

---

[22] C. DE FOUCAULD, Règlements et Directoire, 77.

[23] IDEM, 228.

[24] *Carnet de Tamanrasset*, 188.

you do unto me »... the material alms that we give to a poor person, it is to the creator of the Universe that we give it, the good we do to the soul of a sinner, it is to uncreated purity (God) that we do it ... »[25].

To those who asked how to work in Tuareg circles, he testified:

"It is evangelisation, not through word, but through the presence of the Most Blessed Sacrament, the offering of the divine Sacrifice, prayer, penance, practice of the evangelical virtues, charity - a fraternal and universal charity sharing until the last mouthful of bread with every poor person, every guest, every stranger who presents himself and receiving every human being as a beloved brother".[26]

5. *"Following Pius XI, it is necessary to put in first place, even before charity, the very thorough knowledge of their language, their beliefs, their habits and customs, their culture, in a word the soul of a Muslim. . [...] If we manage to show the Muslim that we take care of him, that we know him in his own language, in his way of thinking, in his traditional habits and even in his folklore, we will be more easily able to force open the door behind which he hides from us. A knowledge rooted in empathy, which seeks the good without hiding the evil, which will try to discover where God could prepare the way of grace and where this grace is rooted to uplift souls".*

Charles de Foucauld studied the Tuareg language in depth[27], precisely to be close, to be able to exercise his charity with delicacy, to dialogue and to be able to enter into the Muslim soul of the Tuaregs. He knows that the study of the language is the only way, not only to prepare the path for the missionaries who will come after him, but especially to make contact with the people, convinced that he will not be able to "do good

---

[25] J. F. SIX, *L'Aventure de l'amour de Dieu. 80 lettres inédites de Charles de Foucauld à Louis Massignon*, Seuil 1993, 210.

[26] C. DE FOUCAULD, *Lettres à Henry de Castries*, 84-85.

[27] At first he considers it an easy language, but as he studies it, he realizes its difficulties and its richness; then, well aware of its importance, he calls on specialists and he will take advantage of any opportunity to collect poems and tales. He will put in writing texts until then transmitted only orally and translate them into French. He will also collect 6000 poems and all this will allow him to compose a Tuareg dictionary of 4 volumes "linguistic work deemed unsurpassable by Berberologists" (Hugues, D., Petite vie de CDF, 119) and which is still authoritative today. He will work eleven hours a day for eleven years and under such conditions as to make his work a truly ascetic task. Cf. A. CHATELARD, "Charles de Foucauld linguista, uno scienziato suo malgrado" in *Etudes et documents berbères*, 13 (1985) 145-176.

to the Tuaregs except by speaking with them and knowing their language".

He knows that by learning the language they will be able to understand one another better, he will understand their culture and this knowledge will create a friendship and love between them, and all this will give rise to esteem and fraternity[28]. So: "The time that is not taken up by walking and resting is used to prepare the way by trying to form friendships with the Tuaregs and by compiling vocabulary, translations essential for those who will come to bring Jesus"[29].

So among the Muslims of the Sahara, Bro. Charles was not a silent "hermit"[30] but a true apostle by creating bonds of friendship to make known the love of God for them and to sanctify them in the same way as the Virgin Mary sanctified the house of Zechariah by carrying Jesus there.

Pope Francis in the last article of his Encyclical *"Fratelli tutti"* says that Bro. Charles: "directed the desire to offer the total gift of his being to God towards identification with the very least, the abandoned deep in the African desert. In this context, he expressed his desire to experience every human being as a brother or a sister, and he asked a friend: "Pray to God that I really be the brother of all souls […]". He ultimately wanted to be "the universal brother". But it is only by identifying himself with the least that he has succeeded in becoming the brother of all." (287).

6. *"In this way we can become friends and speak the language they understand, not only that of dictionaries, but the much more subtle and secret language of the mind."*

To Joseph Hours, a journalist from Lyons who had heard of him and his experience, and who asked him how to be an apostle among Muslims, Charles de Foucauld replied:

"with kindness, tenderness, brotherly affection, the example of virtue, by humility and gentleness which is always attractive and so Christian. With some people without ever saying a word to them about God or religion, being patient just as God is patient, being good as God is good, loving, being a loving brother and praying. With others, speaking of God only as far as they can bear. […] Above all to see in

---

[28] See C. DE FOUCAULD, *Correspondances Sahariennes*, 758-759.

[29] C. DE FOUCAULD, Huvelin, 236-237.

[30] Cf. L. POIRIER, *Charles De Foucauld and the call of silence*, Mame 1936; R. BAZIN, *Charles De Foucauld, explorateur du Maroc.*

every human a brother - you are all brothers, you have only one father who is in heaven - to see in every human a child of God, a soul redeemed by the blood of Jesus, a soul loved by JESUS, a soul whom we are to love as ourselves and for whose salvation we (must) work - banish from us the militant spirit. [...] What a distance there is between the way of behaving and speaking about JESUS and the militant spirit of those who are not Christians or are bad Christians, who see enemies who must be fought, instead of seeing sick brothers who must be looked after, the wounded lying on the path for whom it is necessary to be the good Samaritan. [...] Non Christians can be enemies of a Christian: a Christian is always the tender friend of every person; he has for every human being the sentiments of the Heart of Jesus. To be charitable, gentle, humble with all men: this is what we have learned from JESUS. Not to be militant with anyone: Jesus taught us to go "like lambs among wolves", not to speak with bitterness, harshly, to insult or to take up arms. "Do everything for all to give them all to JESUS", acting with all kindness and fraternal affection, providing all possible services, making loving contact, being a tender brother for all, in order to gradually bring souls to JESUS by practicing the meekness of JESUS "[31].

In this advice there is not only the experience of Bro. Charles, but above all a fundamental characteristic of evangelisation according to Bro. Charles: we are not asked to do great works but to be, quite simply, certain that God passes through us to give to all humanity His grace and His love.

7. *All this "is the application of the word of Saint Paul: 'Omnibus omnia factus sum'".*

Charles de Foucauld's reflection on these words from Saint Paul is: "To do everything with all of you: laugh with those who laugh, cry with those who cry, to bring them all to JESUS. - To make myself available within the reach of all, to attract them all to JESUS "[32].

Doctor Hérisson, a military doctor, who spent a few weeks with him at Tamanrasset and saw his familiarity with the Tuaregs, asked him how to act among them and left us this testimony: "You had to be simple, affable and good vis-à-vis the Tuaregs. [...] be human, charitable, be always happy. [...] Laughter creates a good atmosphere between the speaker and his neighbour; it brings people together, enables them to

---

[31] C. DE FOUCAULD, Correspondances lyonnaise, 91-93.
[32] C. DE FOUCAULD, Carnets de Tamanrasset, 188.

understand each other better, it sometimes brightens up a darkened character, it is charity"[33]

What conclusion for us, SMA missionaries?

1. To be men rooted in the Gospel, to be, as Charles de Foucauld would say, "living Gospels" through a true evangelical spirituality, contemplatives, listening to the Word of God, knowing that "of this Word, he is not master: he is its servant" (PDV 26), through a simplicity of life and fraternal sharing, fidelity, love for the common good, concern for others, especially for the poor, kindness and forgiveness, etc...

2. From Charles de Foucauld we can learn that it is not a question of 'our mission' but rather of the mission of God through Jesus Christ in the Holy Spirit. We are only instruments by which God wishes to be present in the midst of humanity, but it is He who touches the heart of the other, only He who can convert the heart of the other. We, by our presence, by our prayer, in the simplicity of our life, in service and fraternal friendship, we make him present and we give him the possibility of touching the heart of the other.

3. It seems to me that the recent Encyclical of Pope Francis "Fratelli Tutti" is more relevant than ever, showing how to create a local Church where fraternity (or the Church-family) is really the centre of ecclesial life: "Seeking God with a sincere heart, provided we do not use it for our own ideological or practical interests, helps us to recognize ourselves as fellow travellers, truly brothers "(274). It is an existential reality that Pope Francis emphasizes once again: we are all brothers, no one is excluded! The path of dialogue among people of different religious traditions is not just for today, but it is part of the mission of the Church of our time, the Church of Vatican Council II.

4. We must engage more in interreligious dialogue because this is the path of the Church of the third millennium, not to make all religions an amalgam but to create a new way of living together where proselytism gives way to freedom and to the attraction sparked by sincere witnesses through their life of fraternity. To be true to our own identity and without renouncing it, in a world where there are several religions, we are not only called to respect the others but we must also build a fraternal relationship and friendship with them. I believe that all adherents of any

---

[33] R. BAZIN, *Charles de Foucauld*, 379.

religion can offer their commitment to build a true universal brotherhood, to be universal brothers, without making any difference between rich and poor, black and white, north-south. We read in "Fratelli tutti": "It is unacceptable that, in public debate, only the powerful and men or women of science have the right to speak. There must be room for reflection which comes from a religious background, encompassing centuries of experience and wisdom" (275).

5. In the light of this dialogue, it is important today in particular to cultivate dialogue with Islam. PISAI would be very happy to welcome and seriously prepare - as Cardinal Tisserant wrote - those among us who feel called to such an apostolate!

Colonisation and Cultures

Pierre Saulnier SMA

We present here our personal reflections on cultural anthropology, and inculturation in the Catholic Church; we will give examples drawn from our experience in France and Africa without limiting ourselves to them.

We situate ourselves in the contemporary history of colonisation and the worldwide expansion of *Western civilisation,* while making some references to older history; this is the subject of the first part. The second part defines academic terms relating to anthropology and culture; the last deals with contemporary inculturation, including the history of the encounter of Jewish culture with the teaching of Christ in the early Church.

Modern Colonisation

"Freedom begins where ignorance ends." V. Hugo

We distinguish here the various aspects, often intertwined with each other, of colonisation which is not an invention of the last centuries but has existed for millennia.

It is first of all settlement, such as the migration of Europeans to America who then subdue the native populations, secede from their mother country, and import slaves when local labour is lacking; Africa is then the main provider. Or Algeria from 1830.

It is political when European countries engage in violent competition to create an empire. For the 19th century, let us talk of the two Boer wars in South Africa in 1880 and 1899-1902 and the opium wars in China in 1839-1842 and 1856-1860. Crampel[1], passing through Cotonou at the time of its conquest in 1890 by the French army, declares: "I saw ferocious people, ours ...", Later, from 1928 to 1931, it is the insurrection of Kongo-Wara in Gbaya country in present-day CAR; it arises from the exaction of colonisation. The violence continued after the 1939-1945 war: Thiaroye (Senegal) on December 1, 1944, Setif (Algeria) May 8, 1945[2]. Some have not forgotten and know how to remind us.

It is accompanied by economic exploitation; migrants are certainly fleeing poverty, but it is also a question of obtaining products that Europe lacks; everywhere, it's the gold rush.

Finally, it wants to be acknowledged as cultural. The colonized then are regarded as savages, barbarians, pagans, who must be civilized and evangelized. Some even wonder if Native American Indians have a soul! During the first half of the 20th century, "human zoos" are created. They could be seen in Paris, a fenced area with life-size boxes and families exposed to the view of visitors, as in a wildlife[3] zoo. Admittedly, living conditions such as housing, clothing, health care in Africa or elsewhere, a century ago and still now in 2020, are often rudimentary, and need improvement. But do these conditions justify such a judgment?

The Catholic Church and the Missionary Societies are not exempt from all reproach. In November 1919, Pope Benedict XV published the Apostolic Exhortation *Maximum Illud* in which he demanded that seminaries in mission countries provide suitable training for their students. Then in October 1926, Pope Pius XI ordained six Chinese bishops; Rome asks this question: why did it take three centuries to find people capable of leading a diocese when the country is already governing itself?

Paradoxically, the change comes from the colonizer himself; by his very nature, he has the major handicap of his ignorance of the language and customs; he therefore opens primary schools to train interpreters, secretaries, then higher schools for teachers and caregivers.

---

[1] Cf. P. KALCK, *Un explorateur au cœur de l'Afrique*; Paul Crampel (1864-1891), L'Harmattan 2000, 63-6; F. AUPIAIS, *Souvenez-vous. Textes et témoignages*, SMA Sankofa 2018, vol. 11, 73-75.

[2] Émission télévisée de France 2, le 6 octobre 2020, *Décolonisations, du sang et des larmes*.

[3] N. BANCEL – S. LEMAIRE, "Ces zoos humains de la République coloniale", *Le Monde Diplomatique août* (2000) 16-17.

Previously in 1861, when they arrive in Ouidah, Fathers Borghero and Fernandez do the same for the children of slaves repatriated from the Brazil and mixed-race Europeans; teaching is done in Portuguese. In 1864, the king of Porto-Novo assigns them land where they build a house, a chapel, a school. Here too, the teaching is done in Portuguese. From 1868 onwards, nuns arrive to take care of the girls, and to open a dispensary.

What these missionaries, men and women, in education and health do, also responds to the people's demands: openness to the newly discovered world and the need for freedom.

At that time, Father Aupiais himself was in favour of civilisation. In Dakar in 1929, he consoles (?) thus a young midwife, originally from Porto-Novo, posted in Casamance and desperate at not being able to return to her country to be near her parents: "You are employed in the work of civilisation, as if you yourself had been civilized for generations"[4]. For him, this work of civilisation, together with that of evangelisation, is a right and a duty of the Church[5].

Thanks to the schools, these so-called savages reach the level of their colonizers and even perform high functions. In August 1944, the first to join General de Gaulle is a Guyanese mestizo Félix Eboué, governor of Chad; he brings along with him the other colonies of French Equatorial Africa. Finally in the 1960s, these countries gain independence.

It is still a paradox in the field of economics when countries adopt techniques, add their own personal touch and make the countries of origin dependent on them.

I also mention the Beninese Grégoire Ahongbonon who founded the Saint Camille Association to treat the mentally ill. Invited by the WHO to Sarajevo, and questioned on his results, he lectured the specialists: "I am only a tire repairer I believe that you see the disease first, forgetting that it is people who have it. I think you have to be

---

[4] IBIDEM, 70.

[5] F. AUPIAIS, *La civilisation et les excès de la Colonisation*, SMA Sankofa 2018, vol. 8.

interested in the person first before knowing how to help them get out of their illness."[6]

However many others recognize the cultural otherness of these peoples. From 1885, Father Noël Baudin (1844-1887) publishes dictionaries and a Yoruba grammar. In Dakar in 1936, the *Ifan* (Institut Fondamental d'Afrique Noire) is created, specializing in African cultures. In Paris in 1937, *Musée de l'Homme,* is opened - this one is for all continents ... This colonisation thus marks the modern beginning of the meeting of cultures.

Anthropology and cultures

"There is nothing more natural than the cultural."

This saying has the merit of opposing in anthropology *nature* and *culture* and affirming that the laws that govern human nature can only be discovered through the study of cultures and civilisations, each living in its own way.

Definitions

In its French sense, anthropology is defined as the study and presentation of the laws which govern human beings and their different societies, which live out these laws in their respective cultures.

Some are looking for a theodicy, a universal wisdom; at the risk of appearing relativistic, let's say that such a search is a dead end! Each culture has its vision of God, from His negation for atheists, to His incarnation for Christians, it has its own morality, its philosophy, its wisdom.

Alongside anthropology, we find sociology; it studies the human being in his social dimension, born into a family which is part of a group; all research thus has a social aspect. As the object of their study is the same, it can sometimes be difficult to tell them apart.

---

[6] *Terre d'Afrique, SMA Strasbourg 9 (2016).* Review of the sma province of Strasbourg, September 2016. This therapy has just been the subject of a master's thesis at the Ecole des Hautes Études de Paris, by an Indian colleague, Dominic Xavier Vincent, thesis entitled *Anthropological questions related to the care of patients mental health in Baatonou country (North Benin). Study from the Saint Camille psychiatric center in Djouugou.* Note: work carried out by an Indian in Benin and presented in France in Paris: an excellent example of intercontinental interculturality, Cf. Le Lien sma Lyon 575/10 (2020).

Language, too, has an anthropological aspect in the definition of words and the making of a dictionary: it is impossible to ignore the world view of a group whose language is studied. And if one wants to study a people, it is essential to know a little bit of the language.

The relativity of cultures

Like any living being, a culture lives, grows, dies, or becomes diluted by another on contact with it. Each culture is thus both an *absolute* because every person is part of a community that acts according to its own values, and *relative*, because next to it, other people live according to other cultures.

These values compete: a young African skipped his schoolwork for a year because the psychic predicted that he would pass his end-of-year exam. The result was predictable: he failed and understood that he had to work to succeed, another cultural value. How many times in Benin or the Central African Republic have we found young people sitting an official exam without having followed the corresponding courses, counting on luck! Within a culture, especially in contact with another, there is also an opposition between different values, as well as those between individual expectations, including freedom and community constraints, an opposition that makes it evolve.

Every culture is short-lived; we know some of them through the architectural remains, such as Amerindian civilisations, or the Egypt of the Pharaohs and the Pyramids.

The study of cultures

Anthropological laws emerge from the study of cultures. This is the goal of ethnography which is the description of an ethnic group or of a group, both of a traditional, African, Oceanian society as well as of a modern one, such as the Order of Physicians. A second stage is that ethnology which outlines the laws that govern a specific ethnic group. Their object of study being the same, it is often difficult to dissociate them or to separate what relates to one and the other.

A researcher, naturally imbued with his culture of origin, must disregard it as much as possible and not judge according to his personal codes; then he has the advantage of seeing what differentiates his own from the one he is studying. From this perspective, a person who wants to focus on his own culture must distance himself somewhat from it, convince himself that he is not the only one, that there are others with the same objective. He discovers himself in the ordinary experiences of life: by studying the names of birth in the gun environment of Porto-Novo (Benin), confronted by the richness of this oral mode of communication, we wondered about the little interest shown by Africans in this study; Here is the answer: *but it's so natural (sic) that we don't even think about it.*

Africans don't accept the ability of a foreigner to study their cultures but I showed in my Memoirs that on the contrary some find what a foreigner reveals to them relevant and even recuse themselves from prefacing a study, considering that this foreigner is better informed than them.

A fault of ethnographers or ethnologists is sometimes to overestimate the object of their study, as if there were no others, just as valid; some go so far as to claim as the definitive reference and deny others their field of investigation.

Another risk is to limit oneself to obtaining a diploma; even if all that is said is correct, there is still more to be discovered. Completing a degree is not the end but only a stage in the process of learning:

As long as we learn to work, we are young.

If at 20 you don't learn anything anymore, it's because you're old.

He who is satisfied with his business is an old man.[7]

To take account of the different states in the life of cultures, the last decades have created many new terminologies. *Endo* (or in) -*culturation* designates the study and knowledge of culture for a researcher, and for any child who is naturally born into a culture. That of *acculturation* concerns the change of culture, either of a person or of a group, in contact with another. The term *deculturation* indicates the total or partial loss of its culture or of some of its aspects. In the next chapter, we will talk about the Catholic terminology *inculturation*.

In Paris, the *École des Hautes Études en Sciences Sociales* is aimed at researchers who, without an official diploma, can still defend work of high quality.

Some avenues of work

• The human person: the differentiation of the sexes, man / woman, their complementarity in their physiological, intellectual and emotional

---

[7] Reflection of an agricultural entrepreneur in Châteaubriant (Loire-Atlantique), Jules Huard (1866-1933).

differences and their equality in this complementarity. Sexuality, fertility or female and male sterility.

• Relations between individual and community: rights and duties of each.

• Rites around birth, including naming. Who chooses and who imposes the name? The reasons for the choice, and its meaning.

• Education. Who does it according to the sexes?

• Initiation. There are many variants: social, religious… Regarding religious initiation, one should not confuse knowledge with consecration: a person can very well know and understand… without being consecrated to represent the divinity.

• The modes of communication, traditional and modern: orality, writing, radio and television, internet. Each with its values and limits.

• Death and the dead: death of a child, an adult, an old man, etc. Death *natural* or *induced;* the rites around the deceased, the burial. The status of the dead and their relationship to the living. Relations with the afterlife and a possible religion. Regarding religion, it is important to distinguish its foundations from the way it is lived according to people and cultures.

The Second Vatican Council in the Decree on the Missionary Activity of the Church (n ° 26) has a very explicit text on this problem for the formation of missionaries: *"their doctrinal formation must be organized in such a way that it embraces the universality of the Church and the diversity of nations. This applies to all the disciplines by which they are prepared to carry out their ministry so that they have a general knowledge of peoples, cultures, religions, turned not only to the past, but also to the present".*

Christianity and inculturation

Christianity is no exception to these cultural rules. Before discussing the contemporary era, we present how Christ and the early Church faced Jewish culture and *nations*. The writers of the New Testament lived in this culture, with their vision of the visible and invisible world, and their personal experience of Christ; each presents a truthful and complementary aspect.

Christ and His Jewish Culture

When Christ becomes man, Christian tradition speaks of *incarnation*. He then *decultures* himself from his divine condition and is *cultured* by being born a Jew. Then after his death and resurrection, as man and God, he finds his original condition; Saint Paul affirms:

"He did not jealously retain the rank which equaled him to God,
but he annihilated himself,
taking the condition of a slave
and becoming similar to men...
This is why God exalted him
and gave him the name which is above every name" (Philippians (2,6-11)

The important rites of the life of Christ have a religious and often cultural connotation. First, it arises from a Jewish woman, Mary. On the eighth day, he is circumcised, a rite that refers to the Covenant of God with Abraham and the chosen people (Gn. 17,10-14); he receives a name, a rite of more anthropological significance, even if the name is revealed to Joseph, the gospel of Jan 1 (Lk 2.16 to 21), recalls these two events.

The 40th day, like all the firstborn males, he is presented in the Temple, in memory of the Exodus (Ex. 13,11-13). At the age of 12, having become a religious adult, he accompanied his parents to Jerusalem for the Passover. During his public life, he continued to attend the synagogue on sabbath days.

In his parables, he uses images drawn from the experience of his listeners, that of the shepherd, his sheepfold and his flock, that of the farmer, of sowing and of the harvest, that of the winegrower, of the vineyard and of his workers. He compares the Kingdom of Heaven to a royal wedding feast.

His miracles refer to his mission of reconciling humanity with God; for the Jews, diseases, serious infirmities, such as madness, leprosy, blindness are considered as a punishment from God: *who then sinned that he was born thus?* (John ch. 9); in this precise case, Christ clearly affirms: *"neither he nor his parents sinned, but it is that in him the works of God may be manifested" (v. 3)*; and he adds *"I am the light of the world"*. To the paralyzed, he declares: *"My son, your sins are remitted to you"*; the assistants being astonished that a man could forgive sins like God, he answers them: *"you must know that on this earth the Son of man has the power to forgive sins"*, and he orders a man to get up, take up his stretcher and go home; which he does.

While among the Jews, as in Africa, a sterile woman is an object of insults, mockery, the name given to John, the son of Elizabeth and

Zachariah means *"God gives grace"* and he responds to the reflections of neighbours who declare that *God showed his mercy towards Elizabeth* (Lk 1,57).

Material wealth is likewise regarded as a reward that God bestows on the righteous. It is the problem of Job, the rich man, who from one day to the next loses all his possessions and who, faced with the reflections of his friends who accuse him of having sinned, defends himself by shouting his total innocence; but for him and his time, the problem remains unresolved, he does not know where his misfortunes come from: he is *blind*. Christ does not answer on this subject; but he has very harsh words in cursing the rich who *boast of their wealth*; on the other hand, he praises the poor widow who *drops all she has to live* in the temple while the rich man is satisfied with what is *superfluous*.

He departs from the Sabbath law by healing on that day. To the Samaritan woman, he also declares: *it is no longer on this hill or in Jerusalem that you will worship the Lord. (Jn 4,20)* Now Jerusalem is par excellence the holy city of the chosen people.

Even more dramatically he chooses the feast of the Passover to die and be resurrected. Passover, memorial of the passage of God who made the firstborn of the Egyptians disappear, of the exit from Egypt with the crossing of the Red Sea which annihilated the army of Pharaoh, of the 40 years wandering in the desert, and of the final entry into the Promised Land with the crossing of the Jordan. So many *crossings over*! Christ at Passover passes from earthly life to death, then with the resurrection from death to new and eternal Life.

So, it goes beyond Jewish culture; many already believed in a resurrection: *"I know that he will rise again on the last day"* confesses Martha to Jesus in front of the tomb of her brother, Lazarus (John 11). But the Jews do not admit the beatific vision after the resurrection, because for them God is the All Other and no human person can reach Him.

On the day of Pentecost, the Holy Spirit makes one grasp the real identity and function of Christ who comes not as a leader who re-establishes the kingship in Israel but for the whole universe, a non-material kingship, but a spiritual one. In addition, the people hear in their respective languages the preaching of the Apostles; this means that this word is addressed to each culture of the universe through its own language. It took time for New Testament writers to understand and assimilate these teachings. It will be the same for circumcision, the eating of certain foods, relations with pagans (cf. Acts chapters 10 and 11,

Peter's visit to a Roman centurion, and 15,1-35, controversies in Antioch and Jerusalem).

We now come to the Catholic term of *inculturation*, created around 1975; it designates the way in which each community expresses its faith through its culture. It is not just for those who have just converted, but for any Christian who must constantly question how he is living the gospel today. It takes time; a person, a group, cannot suddenly change its outlook on its values, the meaning of its existence, even if it admits the validity of an evolution considered positive. We must also reckon with those who oppose, sometimes violently, these changes.

Here are some examples of inculturation. In the liturgy, after the Second Vatican Council, through the introduction of local languages and music, the faithful no longer *attend* but together express their faith. For Africa, we must add dance, and the Offertory the offering of local products.

For catechesis, Mgr Parisot, apostolic vicar of Ouidah, recommended in 1956 that we should focus *"on the Gospel and on the luminous, transcendent and attractive figure of Jesus[8]"*. But there is better: Father Paul Quillet, presenting Father Jacques Bio Tané[9] who was inspired by the techniques of singers, wrote:

"I attended several times the sessions of singers `that Father Bio Tané gathered. (He) explained the Gospel in Bariba and invited everyone to express according to their art what they had heard. He retained the finest interpretations to flesh out the religious programs he hosted on the radio. These programs were very popular with the Bariba and touched them deeply".

"It was after him that the sma confreres continued to organize such sessions with singers on the themes of the birth of Jesus, his parables, his miracles, the passion and the resurrection. We followed his method to explain the Gospel. We went to (some) villages to have a vigil on the theme being presented. These were intense times of evangelisation where people seemed to fully participate because it was in their culture and in their language". An excellent example of the inculturation of a catechetical method, initiated by an African, adopted by Europeans, to

---

[8] P. H. DUPUIS, *Monseigneur Louis Parisot (1885-1960)*, Imprimerie Notre-Dame 1985, 89..

[9] JACQUES BIO TANNÉ, first priest Bariba, ordained in 1963, died on 07.11.2020, Cf. *Le Lien*, Lyon 9 (2020).

the happiness of listeners, who memorize the text, meditate on it, *ruminate on it,* some would say.

As subjects of catechesis, let us note the very important social relations: learning to consider oneself as brothers (and sisters), whatever the race, the origin. This leads in Benin to the creation of associations of reflection and action like the CPVCM (Christians to change the world), founded in Cotonou by Albert Gandonou, or mental health care centers, such as the Association Saint Camille de Grégoire Ahongbonon.

And again, eschatology and the knowledge of God, of Christ and of the life after death. Among the names of birth in the gun language in Porto-Novo (Benin), I found the name *Mêyisêxue* which means "*Who went to the house of God?*", That is to say that no one came back after his death to describe it to us. For me, this echoes this declaration of Christ to Nicodemus (Jn 8,13):

No one has ascended into heaven
except the one who came down from heaven,
the Son of man who is in heaven.

This is where we will know God fully in an eternal face to face. As for *wisdom* universal, we must refer to Saint Paul (1 Cor 1,17-25).

Conclusion: the meaning of history

Some people are nostalgic for the *good old days,* when the West sought to impose its way of life on the universe. That time is over; since then, many countries have gained more well-being, knowledge, various techniques. They are capable of leading themselves, of participating in the management of international, civil or religious institutions.

Many of these former colonized people have migrated to us, often to meet our needs, so we should welcome them with kindness and learn to work together. They have acquired elements of our culture, but keep many aspects of their own customs and they want them to be respected. It is our turn to discover them; in Paris, you can visit the *Quai Branly Museum*; the *Society of Africanists* offers conferences, book reviews, film screenings. In Nantes, the *Muvacan*[10] organizes traveling exhibitions and the *Maison de Afrique* offers courses for learning African languages. In Lyons, the African Missions created the *Carrefour des Cultures Africaines* headed by an African. These are just a few examples.

We are now living through an inevitable revolution that has been accelerating for several decades. We are moving towards a humanity

---

[10] Muvacan MuSée Virtuel of Arts and Civilisations of Africa Nantes.

that is both unique and diverse, where we depend on each other. Discovering each other in order to get to know each other better, to esteem each other and to move forward together peacefully is a necessity that applies both to civil society and to the Church.

Our
Vision

COVID-19 and Rediscovery of the Custodian Ministry

François de Paul Houngue SMA

(On behalf of the Superior General and his Council)

When at the beginning of March 2020 Italy began to count its deaths by the hundreds, due to covid-19, and when other countries in the West unfortunately followed in Italy's footsteps, the whole world finally understood that the crown of the SARS-COV-2 virus, agent of covid-19, is not only reserved for Chinese heads or Iranian or any particular category of people. Like wildfire, covid-19 has spread across the planet. The WHO had no other option but to declare COVID-19 as a pandemic. In twelve months, its victims numbered in the hundreds of thousands. The million dead mark has been crossed. Even though speculation is rife about the efforts being made to curb the crisis, the end of the tunnel is not for tomorrow, nor the day after tomorrow. Whoever could foresee victory over this planetary scourge soon would be very clever indeed. According to even the most optimistic forecasts, despite the half-dozen vaccines currently available, it would be illusory to predict the end of this pandemic soon. According to scientists and politicians, nothing for the moment augurs a complete eradication of this disease. "We will have to learn to live with the SARS-COV-2 virus for a long time to come": This is the sentence on which the experts now agree.

It is true that it seems too early to evaluate all the consequences of this pandemic, nevertheless the fact remains that we are reflecting on it now in order to learn some lessons from it. Any crisis, even a pandemic, no matter how dangerous, always opens up a vast field of opportunity. COVID-19 is no exception. From our point of view, we can use this situation to revive two essential dimensions of our ministry as missionaries.

Guardians of the mysteries of God

"Let us therefore be regarded as auxiliaries of Christ and stewards of the mysteries of God". (1 Cor. 4).

It is not opportune at this point to enumerate all the evils which undermine our society All the same it is important to note how quickly and acutely contemporary society is becoming more and more materialist, consumerist and very little in love with God. Let's face it, our world is experiencing a real crisis of faith. A fear of God or indifference to God rages in the heart of contemporary man. The faith which lets one be guided by God and his Word seems to be of the distant past. Reason and ideologies based on human absolutism or an 'atheistic humanism' take hold of all human action. The consequences of this choice are not long in coming. This pandemic, could it not be one of the inevitable consequences of conceiving of a life without God...? The question is worth asking.

What are we seeing with this pandemic? We find bitterly that our science-based certainties and ideologies are shattered. Our sanitary systems are breaking down. Our vulnerability is exposed; our claim to dominate the world, like a house of cards crumbles. A little virus forces us to hide, stunned by fear, the fear of death. Pope Francis in his message on the pandemic in March 2020 describes in these words the human vulnerability thus exposed: it (the pandemic) *"unmasks our vulnerability and reveals these securities, false and superfluous, with which we have built our agendas, our projects, our habits and priorities. It shows us how we have left asleep and abandoned what nourishes, supports and gives strength to our life as well as to our community"*[1].

So what remains for us if not the only certainty that is valid, God. What remains but for us to cry out to Him who can do everything? "Master, we are perishing; don't you care? This is the cry that the apostles let spring from their hearts to Jesus who is in the same boat as them, sleeping in the back. Caught up in the storm as they cross to the

---

[1]POPE FRANCIS, *Extraordinary Moment of prayer*, 27 March 2020.

other shore, the disciples of Jesus, very familiar with the sea, think at first that they can deal with the problems by themselves. But their knowledge alone will take them straight into the abyss of the sea and they know it. They will perish. They only have one recourse: to cry out to the Master. Which is what they do when they realize their limitations.

Like the storm, this pandemic strips us bare and the bitter but salutary observation is made - man is not the centre of everything. "Man is not an absolute, as if the ego could isolate itself and behave according to its own will. We are creatures and therefore dependent on the Creator"[2]. We still must return and have recourse to our source. This source of energy that nourishes and invigorates us is none other than the God of Jesus Christ. It is more than ever necessary that we, the messengers of God, are at the forefront of the movement of reconnection to this inexhaustible source of energy. The pandemic crisis provides this opportunity.

Guardians of each other because 'all brothers and sisters'

A pandemic can generate a 'save-yourself' mentality. In such moments, reason deserts the humanity and the basic survival instincts take over, leading to a situation of generalized panic. "In this storm, the façade of those stereotypes with which we camouflaged our egos, always worrying about our image, has fallen away".[3] But our natural state always comes back at a gallop and catches up with us: the sense of being interconnected and guardians of each other. The human person is a knot of connections. The same vital sap connects us to each other. The coronavirus disease pandemic highlights this interconnection.

COVID-19 is the nth pandemic in human history. It will unfortunately not be the last. And the SMA has known pandemics and wars that have marked its history from the beginning. These times of crisis (pandemics, wars, etc.) have often been fertile soil in which the seeds of the word sown by missionaries could germinate. During times of crisis, SMA missionaries have distinguished themselves and demonstrated their ability to work for the good of the individuals and peoples among whom they lived. At no time, have pandemics or wars

---

[2] N. DIAT – R. SARAH, *Le soir approche et déjà le jour baisse*, Hachette 2020, 192.
[3] POPE FRANCIS, *Extraordinary Moment of Prayer*, 27 March 2020.

explicitly prevented the SMA missionaries from working so that the vital sap in each human being can circulate in all.

Bishop de Marion Brésillac and his companions, the first SMAs who landed on the African coast of Freetown, were very soon hit by an epidemic of yellow fever which was raging in Sierra Leone. Thanks to the tenacity and daring of Father Planque, the SMA ship, barely launched at sea, did not capsize. Despite the violent headwinds of pandemics, wars SMA missionaries, acting in a responsible and heroic manner, have never ceased to concern themselves with the well-being of the peoples to whom they are sent and the well-being of their colleagues.

Examples of heroism are not just from the distant past. They are also seen in the very recent past and even in the present. The only proof I want to cite is the decision taken by the confreres, mostly young, to stay in Liberia in the midst of the civil war. During the Ebola epidemic, all the young confreres posted to Liberia and Sierra Leone voluntarily took the option of remaining alongside the bewildered population in the midst of which they lived. Their presence was very active; in a responsible way and motivated by the Gospel of which they are courageous messengers, they used all means, even at the risk of their lives, to provide assistance to the needy. They gave eloquent testimony which has left indelible marks in the annals of the history of these two countries. In 2018, during his visit to Sierra Leone and Liberia, one of the members of the General Council of the time heard several times from the mouths of many Christians whom he met, accounts of fraternal love shown by the SMA missionaries. "These really love us," they said of the SMA missionaries. Their presence among us and their unconditional assistance during the Ebola virus disease crisis spoke louder than the Sunday homilies in the churches."

Times of crisis or pandemic offer the opportunity to bear witness, to rediscover what human nature tends to lose sight of: man is a knot of relationships. This web of relationships makes us dependent on each other. Just as any irresponsible act by an individual can result in the loss of human lives, so any good and responsible act by an individual can save many lives.

The time of pandemic is not the time to 'save yourself'; nor is it the time to close ourselves. Rather, it is time for everyone to say 'I am my brother's keeper' and take actions that protect and save the other. This pandemic pushes us together; together we will overcome it.

"Like the disciples of the Gospel," continues Pope Francis, "we have been caught off guard by an unexpected and furious storm. We realize that we are in the same boat, all fragile and disoriented, but at the same time all important and necessary, all called to row together, all needing to comfort each other. In this boat we all find ourselves. As those disciples who speak with one voice and in anguish say: 'We are lost' (v. 38), we too realize that we cannot each go forward alone, but only together"[4].

In short, the collaborators of Christ have the fundamental role, especially in times of crisis, of reminding humanity of its source which is only in God. Doesn't Saint Augustine say that 'our heart is restless until it rests in God'? The collaborators of Christ must constantly recall the vocation of humanity - to love the other as one's own brother / sister. In other words, the missionary has the duty to put at the centre of his preaching this double connection which characterizes humanity: the connection to the other (the neighbour) and the connection to the All-Other (God).

May we still echo here certain words of Pope Francis in the apostolic letter *Patris Corde*. After long reflection on the pandemic situation, the Pope found it right by launching the year of Saint Joseph which runs from December 8, 2020 to December 8, 2021. Joseph is doubly 'custos': "*Redemptoris custos*" and "*Ecclesiae custos*". He cared for Mary and her Son Jesus. The Church being the 'mystical body' of Christ, "Joseph cannot but be the Guardian of the Church"[5] since he always cared for Jesus. In this time of the COVID-19 pandemic, every Christian in general and every missionary in particular must be inspired by the role played by Saint Joseph in helping humanity to rediscover its Source and its vocation. COVID gives any messenger of the Good News, like Saint Joseph, the opportunity to be doubly 'custos': 'keeper of the mysteries of God' and 'keeper of his brother'.

---

[4] IBIDEM.

[5] POPE FRANCIS, Apostolic Letter *Patris corde* (8 December 2020), n. 5.

Resillience

James Kulwa Shimbala SMA

"When the going gets tough, the tough get going"

The phenomenon of Resilience

This article is about bounciness, the ability to bounce back after experiencing difficulties that might break us. It is also about thriving, not just in spite of the difficulties we meet, but even because of them.

If you throw an egg on the floor it will break; but if you throw a tennis ball on the same floor, it will bounce; the harder you throw it the higher it will bounce. The tennis ball is a symbol of resilient people: they bounce back to life, and continue functioning well, or even blooming, after they have experienced traumatising events.

An example of a resilient person is Saint Josephine Bakhita. She went through a lot of potentially traumatising events like being abducted from home by strangers, beaten violently and cut deliberately (she had 114 scars from cuts deliberately inflicted by her mistress). Considering the traumatising events she went through, some psychologists believe Bakhita should have been psychologically broken. But Bakhita was not just well; she was even able to bring comfort and healing to many people through her listening presence.

Events that can potentially break us today are many: kidnapping, COVID-19 with the challenges going with it (like isolation, financial losses, and stress), excess work due to scarcity of personnel, war...

When in trouble, many people run to the religious leaders, like missionaries. They assume the missionary is resilient enough to face the difficulties of his/her life, and to carry their own difficulties that they bring to him / her.

Helping ministry, like that of listening to and aiding traumatised people, has been associated with the helper being broken due to the weight of other people's problems. It is called vicarious trauma.

We want our missionaries to be resilient so that they are not broken by their own painful experiences, but also they are healthy enough to be supportive to people, without being overwhelmed. In addition to being supportive, resilient missionaries even grow, bloom, and flourish as a result of the traumatizing event. They grow into wiser, holier, and more fruitful missionaries.

After describing briefly the challenges that may break us, in the face of which we need to be resilient, this article will focus on ways to build resilience.

The challenges from which we need resilience

1. Stress

The missionary priest burst out in anger when the catechist asked for clarification. The question was in itself not offensive but it was the last small straw that broke the camel's back. The missionary was tired and stretched beyond his abilities by too much work and never-ending demands.

Stress may manifest itself in headaches, irritability, stomach problems, fatigue, confusion, lack of concentration ... symptoms that are not explained by other biological causes. Stress is a normal response of our body and mind to being pushed beyond our comfort zones. It can come when we are overwhelmed with work, when we have strong feelings that last longer than we can bear, when we have to face a task for which we feel our skills and resources are inadequate.

Negative thinking about the situation or even about stress itself tends to make its signs and symptoms even worse.

2. Burnout

Burnout is symbolised by a battery that has gone flat, no longer energising. It is characterised by constant fatigue, discouragement, disappointment or depletion of motivation. There are often physical diseases caused by the emotional strain, sleeping problems, frustration, confusion, cynicism, apathy, poor performance, and a sense of lacking fulfilment. Burnt-out missionaries may feel sick of the mission.

3. Post-Traumatic Stress Disorder (PTSD)

The signs and symptoms of trauma are diagnosed a month or longer after the traumatising event. They are put in four major categories:

Reliving the traumatic event in terms of nightmares, or even when one perceives something that reminds him of the traumatising event.

Very strong feelings. The reliving provokes strong feelings. Anger can be experienced as rage, fear as terror, and sadness as depression. Some people numb the feelings by taking strong addictive substances, or by acting them out (like shouting, violence…).

Avoiding of reminders. For example, a man may avoid watching fireworks whose blasts remind him of an armed robbery with gunshots that traumatised him.

Being overly alert. Persons with PTSD may be overly alert, hyper vigilant to avoid being caught again in a possible traumatising event. This may mean not sleeping well at night and not concentrating at school or studies. This alertness brings other health and occupational problems.

Examples of traumatising events may be accidents, abuse, violence, robbery, fires, earthquakes, floods.

4. Grief due to loss

Grief is an intense painful set of feelings associated with loss of a person, of a status, of a place or of an object that was considered very important.

Elizabeth Kubler Ross notes that grief is part of a process she called bereavement, which may involve at least some of the following experiences: shock, denial, anger, guilt, attempting to find solutions to the problem even if it has reached a point of no return, sadness, tearfulness, accepting and moving on with life after adjustment to the new reality of the loss.

Without resilience, grief may lead to depression, despair, discouragement, or even to physical ailments.

5. Unhealthy conflict in important relationships

Among the most stressful unhealthy reactions are blaming, criticising, nagging, threatening, seeking revenge, judging, condemning, taking sides against others, and complaining.

We need resilience in order to live through painful relationship conflicts, and to be able to transform that conflict into something helpful.

Building resilience

Humans are rational beings, but not only so: we are also physical, spiritual, emotional, and relational beings. Full resilience has to include all of these dimensions.

1. Resilience through caring for the body

For a long time, psychologists believed that trauma was primarily a psychological problem. Peter Levine and other experts today have proved that trauma is primarily bodily. Caring for the body is essential in building resilience against trauma. Let us see some ways one can do that.

a) Natural release of tension

Peter Levine[1] advises us to heal trauma by following the body's lead. The body is tensed when we are experiencing strong emotions during trouble. The tension is energy deployed to enable us to fight, to run away, or to freeze[2]. This energy does not just go away after the danger is over; it needs to be released out of the body. The natural process is often in a form of trembling. Without this trembling, we can develop Post-Traumatic Stress Disorder.

The following are some exercises for releasing the pent up energy.
- Tension (Trauma) Release Exercises (TRE)[3]

---

[1] P. LEVINE-HEALING, *Trauma*, Full Audiobook, https://www.youtube.com/watch?v=PEf9KI4SWM8&t=236s (Accessed on March 2, 2021).

[2] By freezing, we become paralysed so that we are no longer a threat to our foe so they can leave us alone since we are not moving. Freezing also can help us to numb or even faint emotionally, so that we do not feel the emotional pain of the traumatising event. In that case we can go on surviving, or even rescuing others. Many people who freeze emotionally do not seem to be affected by emotions that would affect most other people. For example, a person who is being tortured may have a blank expressionless face.

[3] This is a series of exercises that one can do at home. They are specifically designed for releasing tension that may have been trapped in the body due to an experience of trauma. It treats trauma without even having to talk about it. Although it is possible to do it at home alone, you are advised to go at least through some training with a person who knows how to facilitate it. Then you can do it later yourself, Cfr. Global leadership team, Tension &Trauma Releasing Exercises, https://traumaprevention.com/ (Accessed on March 2, 2021).

- Capacitar exercises. I recommend the Pal Dan Gum[4] exercises, the finger holds[5], EFT[6], and others in the Emergency Kit[7]. I would need some more theological and spiritual opinion before I recommend some of their exercises like the tai-chi[8].

b) Progressive Muscle Relaxation[9]

We bring about relaxation by tensing and relaxing different muscles of the body.

c) Physical exercises

Physical exercise not only releases the tension in our bodies, but also it helps secrete serotonin, a chemical in our brain that makes us feel well.

We should have at least 30 minutes of exercises four times a week.

2. Resilience through Spirituality

Jesus calls those of us who are burdened [stressed, traumatized…] to go to him and he will give us rest (Mat. 11:28-30). Let us reflect on how religion and spirituality are sources of resilience.

a) Meaning

An icon of resilience through discernment of meaning in life or in suffering is Victor Frankl, a survivor of the concentration camps. From his own experience and from observing others, he discovered that people were more resilient, even in the face of the harshest treatment, if

---

[4] P. DAL GUM, *Capacitar international,*
https://www.youtube.com/watch?v=8CFszXEMlHQ (Accessed on March 2, 2021).

[5] IDEM, *Capacitar international. Fingerholds to manage emotions,*
https://www.youtube.com/watch?v=zC7PSJSoCwI (Accessed on March 2, 2021).

[6] IDEM, *Capacitar international, Emotional freedom tapping,*
https://www.youtube.com/watch?v=_92rfEmXKjA (Accessed on March 2, 2021).

[7] L. CHAMBERLAIN, *Capacitar. Emergency tool kit training,*
https://www.youtube.com/watch?v=nYepPQwtFds&t=57s (Accessed on March 2, 2021); a PDF document can be downloaded from https://capacitar.org/wp-content/uploads/2020/06/English-EmKit.pdf

[8] P. DAL GUM, *Capacitar international. Tai chi,*
https://www.youtube.com/watch?v=r8QgW7-xXxg (Accessed on March 2, 2021).

[9] *Human performance resources,* https://www.hprc-online.org/social-fitness/family-optimization/progressive-muscle-relaxation-mind-body-performance-strategy (Accessed on March 2, 2021).

they had a reason to keep living, a purpose to live for. In his own case Victor had a manuscript that he wanted to see published.

The meaning of resilience has to be larger than our individual self, it has to be positive (not against but for someone). The largest meaning of life can be found in God and in his Kingdom. Saint Ignatius tells us that we are created to praise, reverence and to honour God. Persons like Paul and Jesus even define their identity and goals in life in terms of doing the will of God. Paul says for him to live or to die is Christ.

Victor says that when we meet suffering, we need to give it meaning, "In some ways suffering ceases to be suffering at the moment it finds a meaning, such as the meaning of a sacrifice." He expresses this with an image, "What is to give light must endure burning." We see this a lot in martyrs. They give to their unjust torture a meaning of "martyrdom" or "witness of love and faith in God," and so they endure it quite well.

b) Meditating / contemplating mindfully

Being present in the here and now, body and mind, brings calmness. Spiritual and religious prayers offer good opportunities for focusing on God and on his Word.

c) Rituals and sacraments

When celebrated with faith, rituals and sacrament convince us that a desired state has been realised. Confession relieves feelings of guilt that are common in grief due to loss. The sacrament of the sick brings healing and resilience.

d) Anchoring on a deeper and solid grounding

Jesus said that if we build our life on the strong foundation of His word, then we will be solidly stable even when winds and storms of trauma are raging against us.

e) Embracing the cross

Job accepted the human condition that he was born and would die naked, and so He did not demand that He should always be rich and healthy. This embracing of the human possibility of poverty, disease, pain... made him resilient. When we embrace our cross, we will have only one pain to bear, the inevitable one coming from the human condition, like bereavement. When we refuse the cross, we suffer two things: the resentment against our being bereaved, and the bereavement itself. We can increase our resilience therefore by various means.

f) Forgiving

A lot of healing comes through letting go of the poison of resentment. Drained of the poison, we can be healthy enough to be resilient. Jesus teaches us this by forgiving even persons who were still in the process of killing him unjustly and cruelly.

3. Resilience through management of feelings

In traumatising events, people often experience strong and painful feelings like fear, anxiety, worry and anger. Even though we may despise feelings and want them off our back, feelings are an essential part of our life. They are messengers to us. For example, anger warns us that our values, life, property, relations… may be in the process of being violated and so we need to protect them. Feelings will not leave us before they have been assured that we have heard and acted on their message. What we need is to manage, not to bury them. If we ostracise them, they will come back like rebels and ruin our life and relationships. Ostracised anger comes back and attacks the person's body, bringing illnesses like heart problems or stomach ulcers. It can also make the person irritable, getting angry for wrong reasons, wronging people with unwarranted intensity. Let us see some ways we can build resilience through managing our feelings.

a) Emotional intelligence

Emotional intelligence is the capacity to be aware of our feelings, to be able to name them, to handle them well (instead of letting them control us leading to impulsivity), to be empathically understanding of the feelings of other people, and to have zeal in what one is doing. Daniel Goleman in his book, "Emotional Intelligence" says that emotional intelligence makes us more resilient than purely academic intelligence.

b) Managing strong feelings

Stress and trauma tend to bring strong feelings like rage, depression, dread, and terror. These feelings should be calmed down if we are to be resilient. One of the best ways to calm down strong feelings is the breathing exercises[10]. Breathing exercises consist of breathing deeply, consciously, and naturally.

---

[10] E. COBB, *Breathing exercises,* https://www.youtube.com/watch?v=shryho_PqX8; HRV, *Resonant Breathing Exercise,* https://www.youtube.com/watch?v=DUbAHGPtNM4&lc=UggUUn5D1aYhDH gCoAEC (Accessed on March 2, 2021).

c) Healthy sharing about challenging experience

Recounting what happened in a traumatizing event may be helpful towards healing and resilience, but not always so. There are times when telling the story may cause more harm than good. There are three things to consider when telling the story.

First, the person who is to recount needs to be ready, and feel safe to recount. They should not be forced to tell their story if they do not feel ready and safe to do so.

Second is the creating of internal resources in the survivor. This may be done by recounting with details some good events in life when the survivor felt well, loved, supported, protected… It is important to capture the details and emotions of those moments. Spiritual resources are even more effective. A very important way of creating the internal resources is talking about the safe present moment and place and company, which are safer than those of the traumatising event.

Thirdly, there have to be clear boundaries around the event of the trauma. Trauma events tend to make one feel as if his life is only about the trauma, that there is nothing else. Our current society does not help survivors when it reduces them to psychologically harmed poor victims whose lives are shuttered forever. Helpful listening should help survivors to recognise that there was good life before the trauma, and to identify a key moment after the worst of the traumatic event was reasonably presumed to be over. This then limits the trauma to a specific time and space. It defines the boundaries of the traumatic event as having a beginning and an ending time.

d) Bereavement process

Grief due to loss brings feelings that we described in section 1.4 above. The bereavement process involves deliberately taking time for being aware of, describing, expressing (by talking about them to someone, or by writing) one's experience, feelings, thoughts, acts, imagination, memories, relationship styles, health effects… of the loss. When we pay attention to a particular experience of grief, and express it appropriately, it changes, moving the bereavement process forward, till it reaches a point where it is no longer blocking us from functioning more or less normally.

Common ways of creating time for mourning is going to say goodbye to people we are separating from, asking for or granting forgiveness, expressing gratitude, expressing love, attending funerals or other rituals involved in the process of the loss, visiting the grave, telling the story and expressing feelings around the loss.

4. Resilience through social support

God said that it is not good for a human being to be alone. Adam was happier when he received a companion. Even as adults, we depend on each other for resilience and for thriving. Here are some ways we can build resilience by seeking and by providing social support.

a) Accompaniment

It helps a lot to have someone we can talk with about our feelings, experience, behaviour… Spiritual direction, counselling and psychotherapy are the best adapted ways of listening to us in a way that we feel best accompanied on the process of building resilience. Accompanying people is one of the most important pastoral activities of the missionary. Formation for priestly and for missionary life should include skills in accompaniment, not just education in philosophy and theology. Accompaniment enables us to put into practice what we learnt in theology.

b) Starting / joining a support group

Support groups are composed of individuals helping each other to cope, grow, or even thrive despite challenges. Our communities are to be supportive of the members thus helping them to grow in resilience.

c) Developing and practicing social skills

Social skills like greeting, thanking, excusing oneself, having manners, and following etiquette rules make it easier for others to support us.

d) Giving and receiving help from others

Grégoire Ahongbonon experienced mental illness after being stressed. He was supported by an SMA missionary till he got well. He got even better when he was helping the sick. He designed a method of treating mental illness where patients both receive and give love. Though not a psychiatrist, his method has attracted the attention of world psychiatrists who call him to participate in conferences.

e) Healthy communication

Some people hurt us while intending to be helpful. Healthy communication of what we feel, need, and think makes others understand how to help us best.

Healthy communication that builds resilience in the stakeholders is non-violent, open, authentic, assertive, empathetic, loving, nonjudgmental, and aiming at informing rather than at making someone feel bad.

5. Resilience through healthy thinking

Unhealthy thinking, like catastrophizing[11] aggravates stress and painful feelings of trauma. Catastrophizing is seeing things through an exaggeratedly negative lens, predicting the worst. It makes us suffer from disasters that have not yet happened, and whose probability of happening is really small. Some catastrophiser may die of COVID-19 before even contracting it. Here are some ways we can grow resilience through healthy thinking.

a) Restructuring of one's thoughts[12]

When we catch ourselves thinking negatively, subjectively, or illogically, we should restructure our thoughts. We should aim at healthy thinking, which is characterised by being objective, logical, positive and realistic.

b) Appreciative Discernment

Appreciative discernment helps us count our blessings, thanking God for what we still have, and so we can be resilient, knowing that we still have resources to help us manage potentially traumatising situations. Among the most important resources we have is the Blessed Virgin Mary, our mother who intercedes for us even in impossible cases. I have found very helpful the novena of our Lady Undoer of Knots[13].

Appreciative discernment also enables us to pursue a dream of a better future, giving us resilience through hope and enthusiasm.

c) Behaviour that convinces the mind

There are situations where it is good to worry, and even to act on our worries, for example, when our town is about to be taken over by rebels who have been advancing successfully. Worries are like dashboard lights that point to possible problems that we must attend to. Refusing to act on possibly real danger alerts may just make the worry go the

---

[11] In addition to catastrophizing, a list of other unhealthy thinking can be obtained from: *Checklist of cognitive distortions*, https://arfamiliesfirst.com/wp-content/uploads/2013/05/Cognitive-Distortions.pdf (Accessed on March 2, 2021).

[12] IBIDEM.

[13] For the text of the Novena, Cfr. https://mariancentre.org.au/index.php?option=com_dropfiles&format=&task=frontfile.download&catid=48&id=103&Itemid=1000000000000 (Accessed on March 2, 2021).

subconscious; it turns into undefined anxiety, which wears us out even more.

One way of acting on our worries is to make a 72-hours preparedness portable kit. It is made before the need to flee or to hide arises. Because we have the basic supplies, we can get some peace of mind when we know we can survive even if we have to run and hide till danger is reasonably over. An official government website of Canada offers a detailed advice and examples of items to include in the kit[14]. Include the most essential items like medicine, water, a torch, and food that does not spoil.

Conclusion

Life is sweet, but it is often spiced with bitter and sour experiences. We savour the rich taste of life when we take it with all of its flavours. When we meet the inevitable bitter spices of life, we need to be resilient, to be able to bounce into fuller and better life, for "what does not kill you strengthens you." To be resilient we need to take care of our thoughts, feelings, body, spirit and social relationships.

Missionaries need to be resilient not only for themselves, but also so that they can look after even more effectively the people they live with and minister to.

---

[14] GOVERNMENT OF CANADA, *Your emergency preparedness guide*, www.getprepared.gc.ca; https://www.getprepared.gc.ca/cnt/rsrcs/pblctns/yprprdnssgd/yprprdnssgd-eng.pdf (Accessed on March 2, 2021).

Care for Confreres – Primary role of Unit Superiors

François du Penhoat SMA

This text is a result of my experience with its failures or mixed feelings. I have often realized *a posteriori* to have hurt one or another confrere by my way of doing or speaking. I, too, often listened to the confreres and felt that they had kept a bitter taste, sometimes even a deep pain, because of the clumsiness of a superior concerning certain events that may have taken place a long time ago.

Allow me to begin this text with the praise of Bp. de Marion Brésillac written by Fr. Courdioux[1]:

"The founder was a man so affable, so open, so engaging, who knew how to inspire us with wise, pious presentations, when making his plans known to us, by the uprightness and frankness with which he communicated to us the good and the bad news about our valuable work. Everyone felt, however as humble as he was among his own people, that they nevertheless had their share in the common enterprise, that they belonged to a family whose members shared hopes, joys and sorrows. He often called us individually to his room, he questioned us, he encouraged us; coming out from this heart of a father and an apostle,

---

[1] Confidential report about the Society of African Missions, presented to H.E. Cardinal Caverot, Archbishop of Lyon, April 1878 in P. GANTLY, *Histoire de la Société des Missions Africaines (SMA) 1856-1907*, Vol 1, Karthala 2009, p. 312.

we felt the desire and the strength, for the glory of God and the salvation of men to follow him everywhere, either to both poles or to the equator."

After such a praise and such an example, one wonders what more could be added. It will only be a question of seeing how a person in charge of an SMA Unit can live this spirit today so that each confrere gives the best of himself.[2]

I will therefore begin by situating ourselves in the present day by looking at the meaning of the SMA mission today. Then I will consider how superiors can be attentive to the confreres for the good of the mission. Finally, I will conclude by looking at the very life of the superiors.

I. The context in which we find ourselves

Laying down the pieces of the game before going any further

I am using here an expression of St. Theresa of Avila. She was explained to her sisters how to move forward in the spiritual life and prayer. Using the example of the game of chess, she said that, first of all, one has to know how to 'place your pieces' before starting to play. So, what are these pieces for us and how do we place them?

There is a reality of the world today, that of the Church, and finally that of the SMA itself. The question is to ensure that people who must respond to the challenges that are given to them are in their proper place, feel capable of doing so and have the necessary elements to carry on the 'good fight'.

The reality of the world, the evolution of thinking, of the Church and her way of conceptualizing salvation have considerably changed since the time of our founders. That is why our way of living the mission and exercising responsibility in our congregation must also evolve.

Let us look at the essential features of the SMA mission today.

"To be a missionary from the bottom of the heart"

This is what the Founder tells us - this is the basis of our vocation and of our life. During our time of formation, we verified this desire to proclaim the Gospel to those who have not heard it and it was confirmed little by

---

[2] POPE FRANCIS, Encyclical letter *Fratelli tutti*, (03 October 2020) 3, 106: «Social friendship and universal fraternity necessarily call for an acknowledgement of the worth of every human person, always and everywhere».

little. We made the promise to be a missionary *ad vitam, ad extra* and *ad gentes*. That is to say that we can spend part of our life in administrative or formation tasks, **but we will find again our natural balance in the proper missionary activity.**

One difficulty that our predecessors did not have is the changing context of the world. We cannot live the process of evangelisation uniformly. It is necessary to show great diligence to consider the places where a missionary presence is important. A continuous creativity is also required to respond to the challenges that keep arising.

The first role of the Unit council is to ensure that this portion of SMA lives in a missionary dynamic and to accompany each confrere so that he makes his contribution to this movement.

We are a community at the service of a common project established during our assemblies

I look with envy on our predecessors. They did not have to worry much about how to live the mission. They set out to proclaim eternal salvation knowing that they were 'saving' themselves. They were entrusted with a country to evangelize and they progressed little by little doing it …

Today, it is less obvious to know where we must go and how we are to proceed. The places of the mission are not only 'geographical'. John Paul II spoke of 'new Areopagus'[3] and 'milieus' to be evangelized. Paul VI underlined the importance of 'evangelizing cultures'[4]… The field is immense, but it is no longer the Propaganda that allocates 'a portion of territory' to us - **it is our assemblies that decide about 'missionary options'.** We make choices and we prioritize them. They

---

[3] JOHN PAUL II, *Redemptoris Missio* (7 December 1990) IV, 37.

[4] PAUL VI, *Evangelii Nuntiandi* (8 December 1975) II, 19-20 «Strata of humanity which are transformed: for the Church it is a question not only of preaching the Gospel in ever wider geographic areas or to ever greater numbers of people, but also of affecting and as it were upsetting, through the power of the Gospel, mankind's criteria of judgment, determining values, points of interest, lines of thought, sources of inspiration and models of life, which are in contrast with the Word of God and the plan of salvation. All this could be expressed in the following words: what matters is to evangelize man's culture and cultures (not in a purely decorative way, as it were, by applying a thin veneer, but in a vital way, in depth and right to their very roots), in the wide and rich sense which these terms have in Gaudium et spes always taking the person as one's starting-point and always coming back to the relationships of people among themselves and with God».

become our 'project'. The councils of different Units are responsible for monitoring and developing them. All this takes place within the context of dioceses.

The 'missionary projects' of our different Units

We make them in prayer, trying to work in the direction of the Kingdom of God, where we are. It is a mixture of a dream shared with the Lord and a planning used according to the methods adopted in running corporations. One could say it is a mixture of the divine and the human and we must continually ensure that these projects remain within the framework of the Kingdom of God as Jesus announced it.

It is also our way of living obedience today. We arrive at a consensus and each person directs all his strengths towards the realisation of this consensus. Our Founder was worried about the fear of being condemned for not having obeyed God's will. In our time, our preoccupation is that the proclamation of the Kingdom of God goes in the direction of the Gospel and that our strengths unite with those of others in a great movement of fraternity to carry out this proclamation.

The Kingdom of God is also about giving more importance to the way of doing rather than to what is being done. The dream must come true and remain closely connected to the reality on the ground[5]. In the Gospel, we continually see this interaction between what Jesus announces, how he lives and does and what the listeners understand. This is the whole reality of the 'missionary disciple!

We went from a system of vertical obedience to a collective adhesion to a project in the preparation of which everyone 'has put their hands in the dough'. An important role of the team leading a Unit is to promote this collective adherence to a project.

Process launchers

Pope Francis insists that religious institutes must be 'process launchers'[6], people who attract others to this great movement. He often regrets that

---

[5] Cf. POPE FRANCIS, Apostolic Exhortation *Evangelii Gaudium* (24 November 2013) 2, II, 96, where Pope Francis recalls the importance of engaging fully, till the cross in order to overcome our dreams of greatness.

[6] POPE FRANCIS, *Pastoral visit to Milan: Meeting with priests and consecrated persons gathered in the Duomo (25 March 2017)*,
http://www.vatican.va/content/francesco/fr/speeches/2017/march/documents/p
apa-francesco_20170325_milano-sacerdoti.html

we have the temptation to want to occupy an entire territory by dominating it, believing that we have evangelized it in this way, as in the days of 'Christianity'.

We must live among people so that they may be called and that a certain number, as by contagion, may enter into our way of doing things or invent and start something else but always in the direction of the Gospel. This leads to, firstly, looking to the future and, secondly, to being attentive to see the presence of the Spirit in others.

Launching processes is also knowing how to limit oneself in the work and how to favour the aspects where we can make this Kingdom present in the best possible way. It is also about being attentive to what others are doing and to situate ourselves in complementarity with them.

The role of the superiors in this system is to encourage everyone to commit themselves in the direction and within the framework of this project…

In the service of the local Church

To explain this aspect, allow me to make a caricature of the way of doing things by some religious or missionary Institutes, seen from the point of view of the diocese.

It happens that some institutes come to a diocese with their 'missionary project' that they have developed, and they ask to realize it. The diocese thus becomes a place of exercise or experimentation in their activity. Everyone is happy but sometimes, after a few years, they decide, under the guise of 'restructuring the congregation' to leave. We must hope that the SMA never does that!

We, the SMA, have a tradition of serving the Church and the local clergy. It is by working with the diocesan brothers, by letting ourselves be welcomed by them and by sharing their reality that we will be truly able to bring our charism and also to help them to live our mission better. It is certainly not about competing or giving lessons! When the local hierarchies were born, some of our confreres had to go through a stage of purification, like of misappropriation of the Mission. To be at the service of the local Church is to serve without taking ownership of the land, without being its masters. **Our place and our role will be recognized insofar as we really bring this missionary dynamic to the diocese, in modesty, and without pretending to want to 'give lessons'.**

There are many venues to be used to continue this service toward the local clergy while keeping this fundamental attitude of a continuous, specific and humble presence in an already sufficiently established Church.

The superiors are to ensure the continuation of this dialogue between the diocese and the SMA for a mutual enrichment.

In internationality and interculturality

Internationality is a constitutive dimension of the SMA. It was wanted by the Founder, because of the deep 'Roman' feeling in favor of the universal Church which animated him, but also because he saw, in India and while traveling, the dangers of the Church linked to a political power.

Fr. Planque sought to maintain this view but he found it more difficult to live it in practice, for two reasons. First of all, he saw French food and culture as the universal reference to which everyone had to submit. Secondly, he was not free from prejudices towards the confreres of Germanic origin (because of his French cultural tradition) or towards the Spaniards and the Irish (because of some unhappy experiences). The problems were solved little by little by entrusting different mission territories to each Province, which often coincided with the colonies of their countries of origin.

Since 1983, a great effort has been made to overcome the cultural abyss which separated anglophones and francophones and to move towards an internationalisation lived concretely in apostolic teams and in a continual exchange of personnel. In a world where barriers are raised, our testimony becomes prophetic.

Following the General Assembly 2019, a trend seems to be emerging: the Units and the communities in Mission are led by a team of the confreres originating from the Unit and other confreres from different provinces on mission at the service of this Unit. **This supposes that these mixed teams privilege the Mission and the proclamation of the Kingdom over any ethnic or country-related considerations**. The danger could be that there would be a difference in status between the confreres originating from the Unit who may instinctively see themselves as 'owners' of the Mission and of their Unit and those who come from elsewhere as 'foreigners'. There is an enormous challenge for the Units' superiors: to make sure that each one is at home, whether one originates from that country or not, and that the benefits are drawn from the synergy inherent in this system. We will never take enough care to bring all the confreres together, to revisit the Unit's action plan together so that it becomes a project for all. It is a fundamental element for everyone to give the best of themselves and to overcome underlying divisions in our unconsciousness where some may feel 'owners' of the mission and others 'foreigners'.

Interculturality becomes for us a particularly meaningful sign and a witness in a world which establishes borders. **This continual relationship with the culture of the other, of the brother who announces the Gospel with me, allows us to be more attentive to the culture of the people in the midst of whom we find ourselves.** In a certain way it is our sights focused on a given culture that help us to know it. After knowledge comes familiarity and finally, the love of this culture which makes us look at it through the eyes of a member of the family.

Overcoming our differences of culture or of our origins affects our daily life and obliges us to value others. The superiors must concretely take care that prejudices, as well as *a priori* groupings by affinity, are overcome. This presupposes grassroots work so that the teams experience this internationality and interculturality as an opportunity and not as a burden so that we are then at the service of a true inculturation.

A chain of missionaries

Another richness of our Institute is its continuity. For this reason, Cardinal Barnabò, in 1856, asked Bp. de Marion Brésillac to 'found an institute' to go to Africa. The mission was carried out by the uninterrupted chain of actors. **Our strength does not lie in the fact that we are a large or a wealthy Institute. It lies in the fact that we are able to undertake God's projects without counting time, for a very long time, knowing that others will carry it on after us.**

This requires a good dose of humility, because we see ourselves more dependent on those who have preceded us as well as relying on those who will continue after us. But at the same time, it gives us a great strength to create projects that go beyond us and that will outlive us.

This way of thinking is not natural to humans. There is a great temptation to want to launch 'one's project' without thinking about its future but only of one's own glory. The role of the superiors is to try to overcome the time restrictions that we impose on ourselves and to position ourselves alongside Christ in front of a future that does not belong to us.

The way of exercising authority is no longer that of the past

We do not live any longer in the XIXth c. when the superiors general of institutes (not only Fr. Planque!) appointed and moved their confreres. Obedience to the superior was a part of obedience and submission to God opening the way to eternal life. The history of religious life is full of accounts of novices whose obedience is tested to the point of absurdity.

Our system of election gives legitimacy to the superior, but it is by exercising his ministry with all his heart and by his natural qualities that he will gain real authority, despite his faults and sins[7]. Being 'elected for a time' is an advantage: we know that we have a mission to fulfil for a time and that we will return to another post later. Normally, if we live it well, it gives us a great interior freedom vis-à-vis the gaze of others. I cannot help quoting here this letter from Fr. Planque to Fr. Courdioux:

"You could not tell me better news than that of the change in M. Jean Bouche. I hope he will persevere in his new dispositions. In general, it takes more patience with him than with another one to keep him within appropriate limits; but there is in his profound faith an element preventing him against certain deviations, and you will always see him come back to what you expect of him. Maintain great forbearance towards him and towards everyone. A superior must endure more than another person and often not show painful blows he receives. At the beginning of our Society, I was one day disposed to give everything up because I had too much to suffer from those around me and because I had to govern under perhaps the most difficult conditions I have ever known. I opened myself up about it to our dear and venerated Bishop de Brésillac, and I received advice which, since that day, has made me stay at my post through many struggles. I have had to pass over a thousand things since that time and every day I learn more about how difficult it is to govern. We must maintain a right balance and often lean a little more towards an appearance of weakness than towards austerity. A lot of people have good intentions and they do not take the right direction. Let us straighten them up gently, like a tree to which we provide a support, but let us not break a branch."[8]

The Unit council often has to make 'political' choices between several options after having consulted the legitimate points of view or

---

[7] Society of African Missions, *Constitutions and Laws*, 65

[8] A letter from Fr. Planque to Fr. Courdioux concerning Fr. Jean Bouche, June 6th, 1868.

the people involved. The important thing is to be able to involve all the confreres behind the choice of the council, including even those who were against this way of doing things. Making a choice, discerning, allows us to move forward on a path and to leave others that could have been useful. They were not chosen, we must not look back, we are joining forces behind the one who was chosen.

The spirituality of SMA and that of service

The SMA is not attached to its own spirituality. We can say that our Founders were familiar with the 'French School of Spirituality' through their diocesan formation and the context of the post-French Revolution Church. Let us remember that the Carcassonne Seminary was led by the Lazarists and that Fr. Planque was part of the 'Society of Saint Bertin', a group of priests who were teachers. Both groups had a good clerical formation and took advantage of all the renewal of the Church of France at that time. They were also familiar with the Jesuit tradition – de Marion Brésillac made his discernment with the Jesuits and Fr. Planque put the Sisters of Our Lady of the Apostles under this spirituality because it seemed to him that it was "to be the most suited to missionary life".

Bishop de Marion Brésillac wanted the whole life of his confreres to be dominated by a sense of Mission and a total commitment. This sense of Mission until martyrdom, was the main axis of his spirituality. Fr. Planque insisted a lot on a simple life, without frills or a particular asceticism "because the sacrifices of the Mission are sufficient as asceticism". On the contrary, he wanted to take care of the material conditions of his confreres. Neither of them wanted to add special exercises of piety. They followed what was being practiced in the Church at that time.

But what has forged a certain spirituality specific to the SMA in history is the missionary life and reality, in the sense of Bp. de Marion Brésillac - this chain of lives given in the service of the Gospel. The fact of having seen many sisters and brothers die, still very young, around himself, marks a person and his relationship to God. We can say that, by our tradition, we have a spirituality of sacrifice as pointed out by Fr. Michael O'Shea. One thing that made this easier for them was that they were carried by the mentality and spirituality of the time, like a surfer on the wave and when the missionary had taken the boat, he was more or less doomed to live his commitment! At the same time, the early missionaries saw how the Gospel changed people's lives and how new converts felt renewed by the Word of God.

Today, several factors lead us to review our spirituality while relying on this tradition. We must be open to the Holy Spirit who guides us to discern these places of Mission where we must be and act. We must also repeat from time to time 'yes' to our missionary commitment: **our vocation is based much more on a continuous renewal of our commitment and on an exercise of the will over time to move forward.**

Our spirituality is that of the disciples of Jesus. We follow him in his proclamation of the Gospel, and we live in his intimacy because of the work of the Kingdom of God. In a way, we are connected to him by the same yoke. Companionship in proclaiming the Kingdom and companionship with Jesus is what creates fraternity. As the SMAs, this fraternity lived from day to day takes place at the border of cultures: "Once the Gospel has been inculturated in a people, in their process of transmitting their culture they also transmit the faith in ever new forms; hence the importance of understanding evangelisation as inculturation."[9]

Our spirituality is lived in close relationship with other cultures. It presupposes leaving behind things that are close to our heart: our self-esteem, pride of our culture or our clerical state, etc. **In the end, here too our missionary spirituality must be that of the hymn to the Philippians: the coming down to be in solidarity and to be true**...

The SMA leaders develop a spirituality of service and it is to be hoped that the fact of exercising a mandate of being a superior helps to make this dimension grow. Jesus is the great model. We sanctify ourselves in the service of our confreres (cf., 1 Cor 13,4-7). Our place of service is first of all towards our confreres. We are 'touched' when one or the other is in difficulty, when we are attacked because of our way of doing... But this is how we live an incarnated ministry. And all of this we entrust to the Lord who walks with us.

II. The care of the confreres

Appointments

- **Getting people to 'fit' into the missionary project of the Unit**

In companies, a person is hired according to a fixed job description. In the SMA and in most religious institutes, we do not always get the right person for a given job. Sometimes, the one who has been chosen for a job

---

[9] POPE FRANCIS, Apostolic Exhortation *Evangelii Gaudium*, 3, I, 122.

will adapt. At other times, he will modify what is expected of him in order to make his position suit him, etc. The scenarios are numerous and varied.

- **How do you choose the 'right person for the right job'?**

Each Unit leader tries to do his best to choose the best people for each vacancy and yet we often see some confreres uncomfortable.[10] Often times we have a plan for appointments or a long-term plan to look for peronnel which make it easier for us, but no Unit is immune from having to search for someone urgently because a crucial position has suddenly been found empty.

Let us look at several possibilities (there are others) which highlight this discomfort:

- Some have the impression of being in a position that 'is useless' or does not correspond to our charism;
- A confrere feels manipulated; he has the impression of being a pawn that the superiors move as they please and that they try to reason with him with more or less fallacious arguments;
- Frustration of a confrere who does not feel capable of responding to what is expected of him;

---

[10] M. DE MARION BRÉSILLAC, *Retraite aux missionnaires,* Mendiboure 1985, 108-109 writes: «How many times, in fact, have we not heard it said that such and such a thing is impossible; that with people like those we have, it is useless to try such and such a reform, such and such an institution, and so on? In fact, all that is impossible to a spirit which is hasty, petulant, overzealous and impatient. But let a gentle, peaceful, patient man come to the place; a man who knows how to progress gently, to stop at the right time, even to pull back a little when that is necessary, without weakness or dishonour, according to the counsels of prudence; a man who knows how to suffer contradiction and even insult, responding only with blessings; a man who does not shock and who has sufficient tact to understand that as soon as the clash comes, it is at least time to stop and even to take a step backwards; and you will see these mountains of granite melt at the breath of his kind word, at the gentle contact with his patience. Some days later you will pass and these mountains will be no more. In their place there will be a delightful garden which shows off its beautiful flowers and young plants which will bear fruit in the future, provided that, when the storm comes the man of patience is still there to support them rather than to want to fight against the storm».

- Feeling of jealousy: 'Why am I asked to do this when such and such is left in peace'? What often follows is an accusation of favouritism or of something similar;
- Frustration of some confreres who have been moved from place to place during their life and have hardly had a long enough time of ministry to feel fulfilled.

When we look at these feelings, we see, firstly, that there are some of them that come from the way the appointments were made: in reality, some confreres feel that they have not been consulted or valued enough. Secondly, there are other feelings that come from the inadequacy of the appointment, either for a reason of competence, or because one does not feel comfortable there.

At the same time, when we look at our SMA experience, we see that most of us, we have exceeded our limits and that life has been a continual challenge to do new things that we have never done before or that we would have believed ourselves incapable of doing. How to find the balance between one's limits and this challenge to surpass oneself?

In the Gospel, Jesus sees the full potential of the person by meeting him. It is true when he calls his disciples and it is still true with the rich young man or Zacchaeus. Jesus projects the person into the future, accompanies him (e.g., experience of Peter and the disciples) and makes him pass through a deep personal experience which opens him to a new dynamism. We also see how Jesus continually puts his disciples, eaten away by ambition, in their place and tries to train them in the work of this project which is the Kingdom of God.

From there, we can divide the attention to be given to the appointments into four stages:

1. Informing and involving the confreres in the missionary project of the Unit so that they feel being a part of it.
2. Listening to them before a potential appointment and taking their opinion into account.
3. Helping a confrere to settle in the job asked of him.
4. Supporting him and seeing how he and the position evolve.

- **Making sure that all confreres are involved in the missionary project of the Unit**

If someone is well informed about what is happening now, about the plans for the future and he identifies himself with them, he will be much more eager to make efforts to take on a new position. This goes beyond simple information - it is a 'spirit' that is to be created within a Unit.

- **Listening to the confreres and consulting before making appointments**

When a confrere is approached, which presupposes that it has been recognized that he can fill this position (keeping the up-to-date files of each confrere is important for this), it is necessary to speak with him, to listen to his desires and to see how to appease his fears, if any. Making some concessions (for example, on his arrival date) is always good - it is a small sign that we are not inflexible.

In this listening, it is good to make a confrere talk about what he has been doing and to review with him the continuities and ruptures in relation to what he has experienced until now that this new appointment would imply.

By doing it together, we also realize better the effort that he will have to make, and we manage to perceive his concerns which may reappear at other times.

From there, we can also talk to the confreres about where they intended to go and to give them some indications of how to accept it in the best possible way.

- **Helping the confreres settle into their new position**

First impressions are important for someone to settle down and quickly feel at ease. If a confrere or the confreres who welcome him go an extra mile by being attentive and communicating with the newcomer, it allows him to feel more secure. I remember the 'old' Fr. Arthur Chauvin (1923-1980) who, on the shores of lake Ahémé in Bopa, Benin, showed me the other side of the lake, saying to me: 'When I arrived here in 1947, the bishop accompanied me to the front over there. Then said to me: your mission is in Bopa, it is the village that we see on the other side, the canoe is there, good luck! And he blessed me'. I suspect this confrere of having embellished this story but all the same, times have changed! We can do better without falling into the danger of paying too much attention.

You have to see the practical issues. Often, a small formation can help a confrere to find his place, if one is, for example, to become a bursar of the community - to allow a confrere to do an internship in accounting before or to see that everyone has the means to work without falling into an excess.

- **Supporting a new confrere and seeing how he and the position evolve**

Telephone and videoconferences are useful but be careful not to become 'virtual superiors'. When we visit confreres, staying with them a little, listening to them talking about their projects, their joys and their disappointments, we get to know them better and we can carry them in prayer and understand what they are doing, even if it doesn't exactly correspond to what was expected of them.

By visiting them, we also see how the faithful or people of other religions interact with our confrere and we can encourage him more and in a more precise way.

If this confrere is a little open and dynamic, the work that is asked of him will evolve to connect him better with the reality. It can perhaps also grow with the help of lay people... How important it is to follow and encourage this!

- **Evaluation after two years**

Sometimes, it happens that one feels a certain frustration in a confrere because he cannot respond to what is asked of him. It may be because we ask of him more than he can give (a frequent case in our Units in the Nord where we ask some elderly confreres to do a job as if they were still 40 years old or the opposite, a young person who is asked for more than he can give...).

It can be a result of a 'casting error': the frequent example is to appoint someone to do the accounting in a team while he has no interest or aptitude to deal with numbers... Leaving two years of acclimatisation is a reasonable time but if we see that he does not manage to achieve what is requested of him, it is better to rethink the appointment and, possibly, to adapt an honourable way out so that he can restart elsewhere.

It also happens that someone asks to leave because he does not get along with another confrere(s). In this case, before agreeing to this departure, everything must be done to resolve the difficulties and to restore harmony to the team.

- **Knowing how to ask for forgiveness**

"The boss is the heap of garbage where everyone comes to deposit what they have too much of" (African proverb)

When it is obvious that the team of superiors made a mistake, it is very important to ask for forgiveness. It is a way of removing the weight of guilt that can weigh on the head of a confrere. He will not manage to do his job correctly by assuming the error to be on our side because we have asked him to do this work. By doing that we help him to feel relieved and without guilt.

- **Viewing a new position as a beginning of a new period of life**

When thinking about a new position for a confrere, it is good to look at what it means to him (before the interest of the Unit) and to see how this plan fits in the person's history and taking into account a long-term perspective. We moved from one extreme to the other. In the past, we had some confreres who spent their entire lives in a small corner of the bush; now, we often have a 'missionary zapping' which handicaps the self-fulfilment of those confreres and of the missionary plan of the Unit. We have teams that are always learning the reality on the ground and when the confreres start to know it, they are replaced by others. It is difficult for an SMA member to be truly missionary and to serve a diocese by changing him every two years.

Now, if a confrere has been there for around ten years, it would be good if he went out a bit to take a step back. It might be the time to offer him a *'renewal'* or another service ... For someone who has moved a lot, we must consider how to ensure that he stays at his post to do a real in-depth job. It will also be useful for his personal balance.

- **Mission and missionary assessment**

Perhaps we need systematically, at certain major stages of life, to make a 'missionary assessment' of the life of a confrere. For example, a confrere who has spent 10 years in administration or in formation must have the opportunity to return to a real, pastoral work, otherwise he runs the risk of 'drying out' ... There are times in life when we must look back and refocus our life and our ministry on the mission in order to breathe a new life into our vocation. It is up to the Unit council to be vigilant in proposing something to help a confrere to renew himself. This 'refocusing' requires spiritual renewal and a concrete proposition of work.

Throughout his life, we can hope that a confrere's experiences will assist him to grow, both for the good of the Mission and his personal good.

A confrere inside the Unit of origin or of work

Often, we deplore a lack of identification of a confrere in relation to his Unit. We can, for example, find him having little enthusiasm to do a job for his Unit during holidays, to render a service or even to respond to an appointment that one would like to give him. Sometimes, a confrere has made his life far from his Unit of origin and no longer wants to hear about it. At other times, it is because he feels uncomfortable there or the interaction does not work well between him and the council or one member in particular... In the latter case, it is necessary to agree in the council so that the one who has the best contact with this confrere speaks to him.

How to deal with this? The closeness of the council is surely what helps the most to encourage someone to feel being a member of their Unit. Meetings of the confreres also have a great role to play. We must not forget to value a confrere and to show him the role he plays in the Unit and what he brings, whether as a member originating from that Unit or an incorporated member.

Apostolic communities

A united community is already a potent prophetic sign. But how often do we have to intervene because a confrere arrives urgently at the provincial house or calls for help because he does not feel valued, that his immediate superior considers him as less than nothing, or for questions of jealousy. Sometimes, it is the parishioners themselves who fuel the divisions. If the 'demon of division' is allowed to operate, all the pastoral efforts of these confreres can be destroyed by this internal struggle.

I remember two priests (not SMA) who were both great pastors, have given everything to their work but they did not get along and the parish has gradually divided into two groups, each behind one of the two. It hurt me and seemed like a huge waste. All this capacity for initiative of each of them was blocked and reduced to nothing by this civil war. Often, the rivalries of people are disguised as different pastoral options. I am sure that unity is better than any great pastoral ministry. This is also true about different Church movements. Let us be servants of unity.

In practice, I don't have a miraculous recipe. I know that each of us spends time building unity within the team, but wasn't it already like that at time of Jesus where he had to put in their place the sons of Zebedee or those who wanted to be the greatest ?

Identifying the root of these divisions is the first step in seeing how to act. Listening and trying to bring peace come next. Separating the team is the ultimate remedy, but it will often be seen as a failure even if the person or those concerned will try to justify this fact in another way.

Pope Francis tells us that "A community that cherishes the little details of love, whose members care for one another and create an open and evangelizing environment, is a place where the risen Lord is present, sanctifying it in accordance with the Father's plan."[11] May our understanding, our ability to listen to each other and ask for forgiveness be true signs of the Kingdom!

Make unity

• Within the Unit Council

There is a spiritual experience to make: we are several confreres together to oversee the action plan decided with the confreres and to take care of the well-being of each (and of material aspects too!). We live it with the Lord, but the fact of seeing how to do our best, how to help each one to use his talents must lead to living a real experience of fraternity which will be felt within the Unit.

First, it is necessary to create unity in the council. There is always a 'time for mutual learning'. You have to know yourself and let go of any prejudices about one or the other. To do this well, **one should not be 'stingy' in his efforts to achieve a certain frankness among the members of the council**, knowing that there are some things that are internal to the council and which must not come out (much like parents have their own level of exchange). Times spent together, without special work involved, can help with this.

Another point is the communication of information. It is by having the various aspects of information (insofar as it does not touch a very personal question of a confrere) that each one can contribute his building block to the common edifice.

With regard to what affects people, it is seldom necessary to provide an in-depth answer immediately. What is imperative is to say

---

[11] POPE FRANCIS, Apostolic Exhortation *Gaudete et Exsultate,* (19 March 2019), 4, 145.

that one 'has heard a complaint' and to think how to answer for the good of a confrere or to in order to change a situation.

• Unity in the Unit

When we look at the history of the SMA, we see how much energy has been lost, at certain times, by division, by oppositions of persons or ideologies ... How easy it is to create division and how difficult it is to put everything back together afterwards!

• The SMA and the confreres' families

When I was in Spain, families knew one another, and they met. It's like a big family. In the Province of Lyon, there is no such tradition and the relationships with families change a lot according to the confreres. Some of these families remain very close to the SMA, even after the death of a confrere. Others just move away. In some cases, I got the impression that the family wanted to shield a confrere since the SMA seemed to be hurting him. This sometimes puts our confrere in a difficult situation.

The reality is that we have two families. The Unit leaders can help families feel part of the Mission. In the Gospel, Jesus says that 'his family is not so much the carnal family, but those who do his will'. Mary is the best example of a blood family member who becomes a disciple. I want to emphasize one aspect: this is not only important for the Unit that receives volunteers, benefactors and helpers from family members. Above all, it is essential for a confrere to feel comfortable and to flourish.

We must therefore take the measures to explain our missionary project to the families (for example after the Assemblies) and to find means to be in touch with them over the years.

Major stages of missionary life

Psychologists divide life into major stages, and publicists know how to propose something different at each age. As for me, I look at the relationship between stages of life and ministry. **What is important is to be aware that the confreres require a different perspective and support depending on the stage of their life.**
My approximate (and arbitrary) division has five stages:
- The first five years after ordination;
- The period from 35 to 50;
- The period from 50 to 65;
- The decline 65 to 80;

- Preparation for the great departure (after 80 years).

• The first 5 years after ordination

It is a time of dynamism and movement, but it is also a crucial time. We already think we are autonomous, but we are very dependent on an example. Often, we see in a priest how he copied the model of his first pastor or of a confrere who marked him during the years of ministry. Putting a young confrere with someone who knows how to initiate him well into missionary life is as important as anything he did during formation. This is the time when he can acquire bad habits, a *bourgeois* mentality or lock himself in if there isn't someone who gives him challenges and helps him to overcome them.

It is also a time when we love community life but we easily forget it, caught up in the zeal of the mission. We have a taste for prayer, the seminary is still close, but we easily abandon it for a certain activism. The superiors must be attentive to all this and channel the forces appropriately.

It is also a time of fraternity with the other confreres and of visiting each other. The superiors can help so that during these meetings a young confrere discovers new ways of doing pastoral or other things.

We must be careful because it is a time when, by being committed to community life, we can get into the habit of drinking more than we should or to let ourselves be drawn by 'games' played by some confreres (SMAs or not) resulting in unhealthy relationships with girls, damaging in this way our testimony.

• 35-50 years

It is a time of pastoral creativity. We easily see ourselves as someone who 'does things', but it's also a stage when you can be easily frustrated if you don't recognize your work or if you feel bullied for one reason or another.

It can be a period of easy rivalries. We think we have experience, that we are in control, that we are no longer an apprentice, that we want responsibilities. We easily fall into discussions about ways of doing things, into ideological ponderings or into territorial struggles with other confreres.

Those in charge must be vigilant that a confrere does not 'sink' into individualism and self-realisation in the work.

• 50-65 years

We work, we combine work capacity and experience, but we theorize easily, giving advice without committing ourselves... We can live in freewheeling mode; we can also be a little dictator... The important thing is to live with a good dose of humility so as not to overwhelm others. We must also assist these confreres to keep their dynamism and their creativity in missionary life.

• 65-80 years

We have to face the reality - we can no longer play a leading role. We must leave the initiative to others. This is the time when we struggle with the technology to try to stay in the game.

You can be of great use, 'alongside' young people, but you have to find your place.

• After 80

This is the time when dependency is felt. Elderly confreres can easily appear demanding. Aging means that we need security, and we demand things and we want to get them immediately. The superiors must give the confreres the feeling that they are taken care of, that they do not have to worry about the future. If not addressed, feelings of worry and of uncertainty of the elderly confreres, can create a bad climate in the Unit.

There is also a support to be given to the elderly confreres so that there is something useful they can do according to their strengths. A special attention is to be given to them when they fall into dependence, which can be total.

• As time progresses

Continuing, I would like to list some 'special times' where the confreres need more particular attention. But first, we have to say something about 'ordinary time', about this time when a confrere does his work without making noise and when he does not make the 'front page' of the provincial councils.

It can be good to set an objective to visit the confreres regularly and to try to motivate oneself to respect it even if there is nothing special to deal with. This is important for two reasons. First of all, these visits allow to have a familiarity with the confreres on the ground, to know their situation and possibly their difficulties. Secondly, if someone suddenly 'cries out for help' because there is a problem with health, with the pastoral activities, with the relationship with the bishop or even a burnout crisis, the superior is not an extra-terrestrial who comes only for that.

Special times

I am going to list several types of special times in the life of confreres, which deserve a particular attention. However, the most important thing is that each time when it happens, we transform an ordeal into a time of growth for the person concerned.

- **Sabbatical years**

We, the men of the Church have this privilege that some envy us: we can take a sabbatical and we even recommend it! Our texts (PC 2019) say that this time can be requested by a confrere himself or by his superiors.

During the sabbatical year, there is an aspect of 'great freedom': I do things I want... I take time for myself, to travel, I take some courses, a retreat, follow the ICOF session[12], etc. The important thing is to stop for a while, being someone 'who does' in order to simply 'be': to be with oneself, to be able to assume a new style of relationship with others. We can thus start again in life and be sufficiently available to rediscover the presence of Christ who is at my side accompanying me.

In a way, it's also the time to 'rediscover the world in a different way' because things have changed during last ten or twelve years and I was busy with my activities and I didn't see those changes taking place, but also, because I too have evolved and my spiritual life must be 'updated'.

The role of the Unit superior is to help each confrere to make the most of this time, to accompany them discreetly and above all to take time to listen to them so that what matures in the person during the sabbatical year can be 'reflected' on the outside and that the superiors can bring a confrere back to his missionary life and commitment. The risk would be to think that a confrere who is on a sabbatical can be left without being taken care of. On the contrary, it is a time when we must be closer to him.

---

[12] Inter-Congregational Ongoing Formation (ICOF)

- **Health and sickness**

Before talking about sickness, I would like to say a word about prevention. In the young Units, a growing number of confreres are in the 50s. Perhaps, it is necessary that the Unit superiors organize a regular health check-up for these confreres. Planning those things ahead can save a lot of pain, work and money.

In the event of illness, there are several aspects that must be considered in order to give a moral support to the sick person:

1. Consult the competent people to assess the severity of the sickness and see, according to the means available, where and how he will be best treated. Of course, keep the bishop and the superior of the Unit of origin informed. Think about the recovery time afterwards so that a confrere can regain his strength before returning to his post.

2. Ensure that the work and that which is close to the heart of a confrere can continue and that the confreres of the apostolic community fill the void created by illness. In this way, we can say to a sick confrere: 'Don't worry, don't get preoccupied, you are in good hands, your work is covered by others and you will find everything fine when you get better'.

3. Support him, listen to him, etc. These are special moments when we get closer to our confreres.

Then, we must take advantage of sickness to make it a time of human and spiritual growth. We feel our poverty and we are more real when we are sick. We need to be encouraged to continue fighting so that we move forward, but our poverty is the starting point. Proposing the sacrament of the sick to a confrere is part of this.

If someone is going through a time of illness, it can be very beneficial for him and for all the confreres and the people who live around him: one thing is to accompany the sick, another thing is to find oneself on the other side of the barrier.

Crises

There are many types of crises that happen for which the superiors must act with competence and diligence. If, in the Unit and the diocese, there is a good atmosphere and the confreres are 'followed', we can imagine that we will have fewer crises. At the same time, we must not believe ourselves above these problems.

- **Burnout**

It can happen to anyone and often to the confreres whom we thought to be very strong. All of a sudden, a confrere 'breaks down', wants to drop everything and does not really know where he is.

The role of the superior is not to be alarmed, to judge the situation, to see if there is a need for specialized support and above all to 'take time' of being close to a confrere.

- **Falling in love**

This too can happen to anyone and at any age! It can be a confrere who feels ill at ease in his work or his vocation and that a parishioner wants to 'help him and console him'. On the contrary, a widow or grieving woman who is consoled.

As a prevention, the superiors must remember to 'pay attention'. **Solidarity between the confreres is important. Sometimes, we have let a confrere sink out of modesty or fear of speaking.**

Then, if a confrere falls in love, there is no miracle recipe. We can listen to him and help him to find the best solution possible in this situation. In the long term, the important thing is to help him until he finds serenity. If the crisis is temporary, give him enough time that he needs to recover. If he thinks that it is better for him to leave the SMA, accompany him. Moving him is often not enough to solve this kind of a problem.

- **Ministerial crisis**

It seems to be something of the post-conciliar era but it can still happen today. All of a sudden, a confrere wants to stop the ministry for one reason or another. There is always some underlying cause. Sometimes, going through the canonical process of secularisation is the best way or the only one to reconcile and reunite one's life. For the superiors, there is a whole process of accompaniment to be done.

- **Pedo-criminality**

I listened, in a distant way, to what was happening in other countries. Three years ago, France was hit by repeated scandals. At the level of the Conference of Religious, there were days of formation. I was touched one day after listening to the experience of a woman raped by a priest during a meal. Now, I understand better the deep suffering of the victims. But I was also touched by the account of provincials, in a working group, who had to accompany accused confreres. It is a long way of the cross that the superior goes through living alongside those who have committed such acts. Accompaniment takes a lot of provincial's time and energy.

Caring about spiritual life

In this part, I just want to enumerate some points that are in our Constitutions and that have been emphasized during our last Assembly. There is nothing very new. However, it should be noted that we are in a time of refocusing where we are giving back importance to traditional devotions: that they should be a means of a closer proximity to Christ.

The role of the Unit superior is to tirelessly remind the confreres so that they are to take care, personally and in community, of their spiritual life.

• Personal prayer

We all know that it is important that every day we have a time of personal encounter with the Lord. In the SMA, there is nothing stipulated in a precise way and each one does it as he thinks best. However, I wonder whether by modesty or discretion, we do not often forget to remind the confreres, as they are very busy in the ministry, not to neglect this aspect for their own good and that of the ministry itself.

• Prayer in common

It is very easy to abandon prayer in common. Our Constitutions[13] ask us to pray the morning prayer and the vespers in common in apostolic communities.

• Spiritual reading

It is an ancient means of fostering our spiritual life that we too often forget. It happens either because we believe that we do not have a book available, because we do not have time or because we have quite simply lost the habit of reading. And yet, it is a way to re-centre ourselves and

---

[13] SOCIETY OF AFRICAN MISSIONS, *Constitutions and Laws*, 27.

follow the life, the thought of a predecessor or of a role model in faith that can help us to move forward.

• Confession

We are all sinners! The Catholic Church offers us this means of finding ourselves in all humility and of rereading the common thread of our weaknesses. Let us take advantage of it.

• Time for recovery

We have many possibilities that we do not use enough: time for more or less frequent retreats at the monastery, ICOF sessions, Ignatian retreats, etc. Let us not hesitate to suggest to the confreres to take time out of their ministry in order to be able to keep a balance in life.

• Spiritual direction

This is often forgotten when we are on a mission or we do not take it seriously enough. St Teresa of Avila said that it is very difficult to have a good spiritual director! We can often remind our confreres of it hoping that they will take advantage of it seeing it for what it really is – something that we need.

• Beware of chastity

Chastity is often reduced to celibacy but it is a whole balance of our relationships that is at stake. It concerns our way of giving ourselves to others. Often, we have a lot of relationships, but they are superficial. Sometimes, it is a lack of a real brotherhood between us or a suspicion about others that makes us to become more centred on ourselves.

Chastity and interculturality are dimensions of our life that affect our spirituality. Our ability to relate to others, to the most underlying and instinctive aspects of our person: the spiritual and the human, what is most basic, come together in the encounter with the other who is different, because of a different gender or culture. We can become a person who helps others to feel better or a person trapped in his feelings who is afraid and who withdraws into himself.

At the same time, we must not forget that the relationship to chastity evolves and I hope it matures with the experience and with years. Having some older confreres in our teams helps to experience this as a process.

Cultivating a well-lived chastity is also learning a true compassion, which "did not make him hesitant, timid or self-conscious, as often happens with us. Quite the opposite."[14] It is to feel what others experience and let ourselves be affected by these feelings without being upset but bringing them to the Lord. At the end of the day, it's difficult to strike a balance but it is what helps us to be ourselves, that strengthens our personality and that puts it at the service of others.

The superiors must be attentive to the general atmosphere of the communities and to see how each one really commits himself "from the bottom of his heart" to the Mission. Perhaps we need to create some spaces of deep sharing where we can say things that will do good to each of us, using a biblical or spiritual text as a starting point...

III. The spiritual life of SMA Superiors

This title appears very pretentious! I will begin by making a list of the superiors' temptations as I see them. Of course, this list is not exhaustive! I hope that it will enable us to help each other to make the examination of conscience. Then, I will enumerate some virtues to cultivate...

The temptations of the superior

In relation to his Unit
- Believing oneself the owner and not a steward;
- Thinking of oneself as the only one having the Holy Spirit;
- Wanting to do a great work that will last.

In relation to the confreres
- Acting by manipulating one or the other;
- Wanting to divide in order to rule.
- Lying.

In relation to oneself
- Depending very strongly on the image that one wants to project for others;
- Wanting to avoid suffering and difficulties;
- Allowing oneself to be overcome by weariness or fatigue.

---

[14] POPE FRANCIS, Apostolic Exhortation *Gaudete et Exsultate,* 4, 131.

The virtues to cultivate among those who are in charge

I am just going to outline a few points by referring the reader to the apostolic exhortation of Pope Francis *"Gaudete et Exsultate"* in its fourth and fifth chapter (n°. 110-177).

- **Discernment**

  As we have already seen, to contemplate the reality in which we live, to see the places where the demon acts with a certain ease to confuse our minds, to recognize the action of the Spirit in the world, all of this requires vigilance and an awaken spirit as Jesus himself points out several times in the Gospel. For us, it is the first step in knowing where to situate ourselves and how to act.[15] This is particularly true for areas that we consider to be 'Christianized', and where some very strong expressions of paganism keep emerging, or in the West (and in the ideology of globalisation) where we present an ideology as the natural and supreme good.

  Choosing is part of the superiors' job. Being able to do it with a certain independence of mind and in prayer allows us to make a choice with the strong enough feeling that we are going in the direction indicated by God. This helps us to make inner freedom a freedom of action. **God gives us great freedom in our action. May he support the options that we take, may he continuously help us to get the good out of an error.**

  No one has the Spirit alone! It is also by consulting specialists in the areas that we are not familiar with, and by thinking together inside the council that we manage to do something.

  This is especially true for a lot of material or financial matters which have become, in most cases, very complicated and beyond our competence. Knowing how to surround yourself with right people is an art. A good, devoted Christian is not always a good technician!

- **Humility**

  In the SMA, many things push the superior towards humility: the dire frankness with which the confreres express their opinion or their disagreement, the short duration of a mandate to do something (not to mention the short duration of our life!); our own limitations.

---

[15] It concerns the practical application of the meditation about two kingdoms by St. Ignatius of Loyola

And yet, the temptation to want to be a 'leader' is great: to want to show our authority and to want to believe that we are the holders of a 'power'. There is a strong temptation to want to avoid anything that demeans us.

Quite often the demon makes us believe that we are important and pushes us to show this importance by external signs, by our way of speaking or acting. He invites us to believe that we are more far-sighted than others and thus leads us astray. Sometimes, this error consists in looking down on others, in adopting a posture of a ruthless judge that leads us to a certain violence towards our confreres.

Humility and truth go together. If we experience real humility, we will create a climate of truth in our Unit and we will grow ourselves in humanity. Humility goes with the cross and we must learn to familiarize ourselves with it. It is a way of being that we learn little by little and will be learning it until the grave.

- **Perseverance**

Which one of us has not had, at one time or another, a desire to give up, to resign, or to go and take another post because a confrere told us that what we were doing was meaningless or that we had not done something well. And yet, it is in perseverance that we serve the Kingdom of God.

We have the model of perseverance in Fr. Planque: 50 years of ceaseless struggles in the service of the SMA so that it continues and is not 'swallowed' by some ambitious people, or does not become a toy of a group inside the congregation.

Perseverance is, first of all, this fight within ourselves, with our weaknesses, with our sins but it is also a fight against the devil who wants to hinder the progress of the Kingdom of God. Pope Francis explains it well when he insists that the power of the Evil One is among us and therefore it has such a destructive impact[16]. But it is above all the fight alongside Christ so that the Kingdom of God may be present.

---

[16] POPE FRANCIS, Apostolic Exhortation *Gaudete et Exsultate*, 5, 160.

"The joy I wish you"

We all know this sentence from Bp. de Marion Brésillac! To be happy where the Lord has placed us, to be happy to do one's job and to do it in the best possible way, to be happy to be with other brothers and sisters.

If we, the superiors of an SMA Unit, are not happy, how will we make others happy? The proclamation of the Gospel is a Good News that is lived and transmitted by more by a deep and peaceful joy that we will manifest rather than by great speeches.

Watch out for a fake joy! It is by living love to the end that we will be able to show this true and profound joy of a life united in the service of the Kingdom of God.

In concluding this text, I have the impression of having said a lot of things and I remember a Bariba proverb: 'Words without deeds are worth nothing'. No one can be perfect. I also know that there are many ways of doing things. It is up to everyone to consider, with their own nature and talents, within the context of the Unit in which they live, how to ensure that harmony and peaceful joy of missionaries reign.

May the Lord accompany each of us!

Care for Members

Fabien Sognon SMA

I would like to begin my presentation by quoting the 1983 Code of Canon law Canon. 619: "Superiors are to devote themselves diligently to their office and together with the members entrusted to them are to strive to build a community of brothers or sisters in Christ, in which God is sought and loved before all things. Therefore, they are to nourish the members regularly with the food of the word of God and are to draw them to the celebration of the sacred liturgy. They are to be an example to them in cultivating virtues and in the observance of the laws and traditions of their own institute; they are to meet the personal needs of the members appropriately, solicitously to care for and visit the sick, to correct the restless, to console the faint of heart, and to be patient toward all." This provision by the canon law imposes certain obligations on superiors in terms of taking care of their members. Since the wellbeing of members is entrusted to superiors by God, the exercise of this duty must be seen as a pastoral service. This implies that the care to be given must go beyond the social or the physical. It must necessarily touch on the spiritual, the salvation of members.

Again, this provision prompts us to strike the balance between administration and spiritual leadership. Administration concerns the normal paper or office work whereas the spiritual services are about community life in relation to our prophetic role of announcing the Kingdom.

Administrative work	Spiritual leadership
Immigration papers	Retreats
Health	Recollections
Food and drink	Spiritual direction
Tyrocinium	Spiritual books
Holidays	Fraternal unity
Retirement	*(cf. GA 19 nos. 53.2-56.2)*
Bereavement	
Crisis and trauma`	

1. Administrative functions

I will dwell on this aspect since the other part (spiritual roles) is clear enough. Many documents on the spiritual roles of leaders exist to help superiors.

The superiors must ensure the following:
- Members should enter their countries with the right visa
- Appropriate residence permits are obtained
- The yearly (periodic) renewal of residence permit is done
- Remind members to renew their permits since they can forget
- Make sure people are informed about specific cultural realities in order to avoid them being shocked, and about particular subjects which every visitor should avoid so as not to create problems later on.
- Explain how things are organized and everything else that a newcomer should know from day one.

2. Health

Heath is paramount. Superiors have a big role in both preventive and curative care.

Preventive care includes: regular check-ups; each member has to listen to be alert to his own state of health; what he can take which will not harm him, and what he likes but must avoid.

A special reminder to those suffering from blood-pressure, diabetes, heart issues and other underlying health conditions. It is also important to educate members on the consequences of some dangerous practices such as excessive alcohol consumption, smoking or drink-driving. This aspect also affects health insurance. The EMI or any type of health insurance must be updated regularly for those in Africa and those outside Africa should be under a good health insurance package. The superior must collaborate with the bursar in updating the list.

Curative care: This is when the person is already sick and needs attention.

When this occurs, superiors must play a leading role in the treatment process by finding the appropriate health facility and liaising with the medical experts to ensure good care. All Units should have a realistic financial plan for possible cases. Health care can be one of the biggest expenses. A list of specialist (dentists, ophthalmologists, ORL), hospitals and other health care facilities can be compiled in each Unit for use by members because some health services are fully covered by EMI while others are not.

3. Food and drink

Food and drink are important for our survival. Members must eat healthy and balanced meals to keep well. It is therefore the duty of the superiors to ensure that the following are in place:

That communities provide good food for members and superiors must enquire about the standard of meals when they visit communities or parishes. Not only Nutritious food should be provided all the time, not only when the superior is around.

Regular evaluation of the food provision in every community.

For instance, while visiting communities, superiors could bring some food items that are hard to find in rural areas. They could also donate good wine for Christmas or Easter celebrations, as some superiors, who shall be nameless, have always done!

4. Tyrocinium and regular meeting

"The Unit Superior organizes an orientation program related to the country's historical, socio-political, cultural and religious realities for newly appointed SMA members and associates in his Unit." GA 19 no.147. "Superiors invite experts from the civil society (sociologists, anthropologists, psychologists, political scientists, etc.) to help members understand the changing situation of the world so as to re-adjust our missionary activity. Unit Superiors provide a budget for seminars and workshops organized on relevant topics and ensure that members take part." (AG 19 no.158). This section concerns the training and updating of pastoral agents in line with the ever changing realities of the country and of the wider world. To be effective in his ministry, a missionary or any pastoral agent must have a close and deep contact

with the milieu and the people he is appointed to minister to. This program is there to help the missionary to explore the various levels of **See, Judge and Act** of pastoral theology. A missionary attuned to his world and his God. It is the best way to make the Gospel take deep root in the life of people. (*Redemptoris Missio* 31-38; 52-54; *Pastores Dabo Vobis* 5-7; 57-59; 71-77; 80-81)

The superiors must also keep regular contact with all the members through various means of communication... Such efforts demonstrate closeness to the members and some news can be shared outside of the regular meetings and everyone is kept updated on the news of each place and confrere.

5. Holidays

When members are on holidays, superiors have the fatherly duty of welcoming them, therefore they should inform them earlier of their coming. Members also need to plan their stay in conjunction with their superiors so that they can be properly provided for. To those who are entitled to it, allocation is given. Again the duties and rights of everybody are well clarified (defined).

6. Retirement

At the moment we from the younger Units do not have any retired members so my suggestions at this stage will be centred on activating the preparations plans. We propose the setting up of a progressive plan to be implemented on retirement for those are eligible including putting up suitably adapted buildings. We may have to draw up quite a detailed plan. But it is better to start thinking of it now because old age is just around the corner. The key to facing it with serenity is good planning, investigating some possibilities and even undertaking some projects designed for 20 years further in the future.

7. Bereavement

This is a sensitive time for members so they must experience truly the SMA family love. It is a time when superiors must be really close to the bereaved member.

When members lose their biological parents, a small financial support is given to the person in accordance with African customs.

- Organize confreres to attend the funeral of deceased family members
- Show support to the members in various ways if possible. I have personally taken part in some funerals of confrere's parents where I presided over the burial mass and the final commendation rites.
- If it is a confrère, take the immediate necessary measures
- Inform the bishop of the diocese, see to all the administrative requirements
- Arrange for an appropriate burial site in case nothing had been stipulated before.

8. Crisis and trauma

Members can experience difficult emotional and psychological moments while on mission. Some can be due to war, physical attacks, armed robbery or difficult community life in some extreme cases. We all go through different crises from time to time. There are difficulties that can become more serious and can impact negatively on our ability to love or to act. Leaders, as well as confreres who know about the situation, need to support the member in crisis in order to help him, to understand his difficulties and anticipate his possible reactions and reassure him.

About our confreres

Behind every difficult situation a confrere may be suffering and we need to do our best to understand. What has been the cause or what has led this confrere to this difficult situation? What has been his personal story, his formation, his relationship with other confreres? What have been his personal ministries, his missionary activity, his hopes, his crises, his struggles, his victories, and his failures? It is not easy to get answers to these questions, but they can help us understand the situation he might be going through. Confreres who go through difficulties such as disappointment burn-out from a particular task, physical, psychological or affective illnesses or difficulties with their spiritual life deserve our support, solidarity and respect, so as to help them carry their heavy burdens.

Another aspect we should not forget is the type of confreres who are called the "Present but Absent". They are appointed to a particular place or task but are spiritually, physically, and emotionally absent. Sometimes they have a negative impact on others. Some live practically in isolation.

Preventive measures

Superiors must support members in difficult moments and promote good community life. People should be encouraged to communicate about issues frankly and if they do not superiors must try to find a way to initiate dialogue with them and allow them to open up. It is important to foster good relationships that will allow everyone to express himself and seek help if needed. It helps to have moments of relaxation and time to exchange views at table without offending anyone

Curative measures

- Leaders and all those involved in the treatment and care of the members must observe great confidentiality. Everyone has the right to their good name. There should be no divulging of the member's situation. Sensitive matters should be treated with discretion and the one going through such a situation needs to be told not to be ashamed or afraid to speak frankly but be reassured by the atmosphere he feels around him.

- Professional assistance should be sought for the member.

- Records of the member's treatment should be destroyed or kept outside of his personal file. Again, we all have the right to our good name. Discretion regarding sensitive issues should be paramount out of respect for the members.

- Other crises might include various moral issues. Different types of accusations have to be handled carefully and with respect towards the individual implicated, whether truly or falsely.

It is important to make financial provision for unforeseen problems. Not everybody has the wherewithal to deal with the costs that these might incur but good financial planning is the key to being able to react appropriately when these crises occur. Sometimes, there can be more than usually expensive health problems, and we must be ready to face the difficulties and resolve them.

Leaders are invited to carry out this type of care in a spirit of fraternal love. The person who has been rescued from a difficult situation should not be made to feel that he owes a moral debt to the superior as an individual. Such a situation, if not attended to, may lead to an unhealthy dependency.

House Built for Storms

S. I. Francis Rozario SMA

For the first time in our lifetime, we stand face to face with a full-blown pandemic that has defied the entire world and has already moved well into the second year as we publish this bulletin. Everybody scrambles to make sense of the undeniable, unignorable and unescapable reality we are going through.

Compelling times to test and adjust our basic convictions about life.

In the first part of this article, we will focus on a few popular ways of understanding and interpreting misfortunes in life, analyse them critically, and expose their limits. In the second part, we will walk with Jesus and see how he interprets similar events when he comes across them. Then in the third part we will make a synthesis of the Christian convictions regarding storms in life.

I. Making sense of misfortunes

Life-threatening dangers and disasters stay like dark clouds over the head. No one knows what will strike whom and when. Let us explore certain ways of reasoning and their roots in the Old Testament and in Asian and African cultures.

Old Testament

The Bible is the word of God written by human authors as they understood it. This explains not only the differences but also the evolution in theology in the same Bible. We see significant changes and growth in the understanding. Make no mistake, a new understanding sits close to the older ones without replacing them.

I am special and I do not suffer

Abraham, the father of faith goes through an amazing, powerful, and eye-opening God experience. He feels in his heart and gut the love and providence of God. He realises how precious he is in the sight of God. That enables him with absolute trust and confidence to obey God. He has no doubt, God is at his side. We read the promise of God to Abraham in Genesis 12:1-3 *"¹Go from your country and your kindred and your father's house to the land that I will show you.²I will make of you a great nation, and I will bless you, and make your name great, so that you will be a blessing. ³ I will bless those who bless you, and the one who curses you I will curse; and in you all the families of the earth shall be blessed."* God gives a command in verse one and quite a few promises in the following verses. God promises a general blessing for the life of Abraham in verse two and then we see something extraordinary in verse three *"I will bless those who bless you, and the one who curses you I will curse"*. We surely need to dig more deeply here.

The common blessing goes like this: "Blessed are those who bless you and cursed are those who curse you". We see that in the blessings given to Jacob (Gen 27:29) and Judah (Num 24:9). Note two major changes in the blessing of Abraham. The personal direct involvement of God is emphasised with the use of the first-person pronoun (**I** will bless ... **I** will curse) replacing the impersonal form of the popular saying (blessed are … cursed are).

The second change disappears in many translations. Two different verbs are used in Hebrew for curse. The verb used for the one who curses Abraham (qalal) is much lighter and could be translated as 'despises, disdains, disrespects' and the verb used to curse that person (arar) is very strong.[1] We can translate the verse as 'I will CURSE anyone who despises/disdains/disrespects you'. It is like saying, 'I will deal harshly with anyone who touches you'. This statement shows a tremendous sense of self-esteem.

Abraham feels empowered by this realisation, fearlessly leaves his father's country and ventures into an unknown territory.

The patriarchs shared the faith convictions of Abraham. Abraham, Isaac, and Jacob lived long and possessed enviable amounts of wealth with a lot of animals, servants, and slaves. Added to that they had beautiful wives. The irresistible beauty of Sarah and Rebecca even got

---

[1] G. J. WENHAM, *Word Biblical Commentary*, Vol. 1, (Dallas: Word, Incorporated, 1987), 276.

them into serious trouble (Gen 12:10-20, Gen 26: 6- 11). Though barren (Gen 16:1-2 (Sarah), 25:21 (Rebecca), 29:31 (Rachel), they bore children by the special grace of God. In short, the patriarchs had everything desirable and lacked absolutely nothing. They were spared from misfortunes. We can summarise the overall understanding as follows:

- Abraham was chosen by God as a special privileged person.
- He obeyed God and God blessed him
- Blessing means riches, long life and descendants which become possible as those considered blessed are saved from all misfortunes.

My God fights for me and I do not suffer

We read about several wars in Deuteronomistic history (Joshua, Judges, 1,2 Samuel and 1,2 Kings). Fortunately, we do not find all the details in our lectionary. That makes life a bit easier for preachers. What disturbs more than the gruesome and disgusting war details is the underlying theological conviction. For example, the first king of Israel, Saul is discredited not because of any war-crime but because he did not kill the captured king Agag and did not destroy all the sheep and cattle of Amalekites!!! Saul pleads guilty and seeks pardon!!! What happens then to King Agag? Samuel the prophet finishes the job Saul, the warrior king failed to do. Where? In the sanctuary 'before the Lord in Gilgal' (1 Sam 15:10-34).

This is just one of the many similar instances of the so called 'Herem' - 'devoted to destruction' (Cf. Lev 27:28-29, Josh 6:17, 8:26, 1 Ki 20:42). Though horrible and sickening, it goes perfectly in line with the theological understanding seen in the final discourse of Joshua:

"³ You have seen all that the LORD your God has done to all these nations for your sake, for it is the LORD your God who has fought for you. ⁶ Therefore be very steadfast to observe and do all that is written in the book of the law of Moses, [...] ⁷ so that you may not be mixed with these nations left here among you, or make mention of the names of their gods, or swear by them, or serve them, or bow yourselves down to them, [...] ¹² For if you turn back [...] ¹³ know assuredly that the LORD your God will not continue to drive out these nations before you; [...] until you perish from this good land that the LORD your God has given you."
(Joshua 23:3-13)

Let us outline the convictions:

- *'Our'* god protects *'our'* people. He has nothing to do with 'other' people who have 'their' gods.
- When we go to war, our god comes with us, fights for us against 'others'. Sparing an enemy in war betrays god who did his part in the battle.
- When we win, it shows the greatness of our god compared to the gods of other people.
- We lose either because the other gods were stronger or because our god did not come with us. We had to go for war alone without our god who is annoyed with us for one reason or the other. Most often it is because some people admired and followed other gods.

As long as I serve my god, he will fight for me and I will not suffer.

I am good I will not suffer throughout my life

The book of Job discusses the polemic of the suffering of a just person. Job lived an impeccable life and avoided evil beyond any normal standard. He offered sacrifices of reparation not for his known sins or those of his children but for the possible sins and blasphemies his children might have committed in their thoughts, not even in their actions. This was the extreme extent of his righteousness. A man with this record should not suffer but is devastated and goes through a terrible agony. The book discusses the shocking and dramatic details of the misfortunes and the reasoning of people.

At the end of the book, Job is vindicated. His regains health and wealth including children during his lifetime. The book of Job tolerates a short-term suffering for a just man and the person is vindicated during his own lifetime.

Some Asian and African interpretations

Asia

In the whole discussion on evil, people find the sense of justice quite intriguing and even worrying. People do not mind suffering provided they see some logic in it. They compare their sufferings with those of others to understand justice and fairness. For example, when everybody who studies hard gets good marks and secures a good job, the suffering involved does not look like suffering at all. It can be taken as the normal process. How come some suffer far more than the others? How is it fair and just? Is there any logic behind?

Life presents different challenges and opportunities to different people depending on their physical and mental conditions, the social and financial status of their families, and their gifts and limitations.

Indian philosophy believes strongly in justice and fairness and it sees no possibility for justice in a single cycle of life. People finish their entire life without enjoying the fruits of their virtues and without paying penalties for their vices. Mere death cannot reset our accounts to zero. People need to reincarnate and have many cycles of life till all accounts are settled. The bottom line is that everybody must pay for his / her actions sooner or later.

How do we see suffering in this framework? You suffer because you are paying for the sins of your last life or because of the evil of somebody else for which the evil doer will be punished during this life or in the next, and you will be vindicated either during this life or in the next.

Africa

Many African cultures deeply love life in its fullness and believe that only good and pleasant things are natural and unpleasant things are provoked by bad intentions. This conviction unveils a wonderful truth. Goodness can exist by itself. Evil is not necessary for life. Evil itself has no independent existence; it is nothing but the absence of good.

Many African cultures celebrate life and explicitly deny that sickness and death can be natural or normal. However, despite the denial, we have no option but to face sickness, problems, and death day after day.

Social implications of these convictions

Many good Christians including priests and religious share and promote the convictions discussed above. Apart from being unsatisfactory and inadequate, they sow poisonous seeds in the society. Let us see how.

1. I am special, and I do not suffer, or I should not suffer

The closer we look at this mindset, the more frightening it appears. This belief makes one totally oblivious to the suffering of others and gives a sense of entitlement denying any hint of equality. One can even be proud of getting benefits at the expense of others and worse, can thank God for that. Good believers can sit comfortably in a messy situation without doing anything to improve it just because they are not directly touched. A road can be bad causing regular accidents and people can thank God for their safe journeys without becoming scandalised by the constant deaths of people.

The same people will feel terribly scandalised when they are confronted by the conditions everybody else has to deal with. Many Christians were shocked and scandalised when they learnt that priests and bishops succumbed to the Corona virus.

Is it not childish, insensitive, and selfish to wish that only I should be spared and treated with privileges? Childish convictions seem harmless in children but prove terribly dangerous in adults. Fundamentally this sense of entitlement goes against solidarity, equality, and compassion – essential blocks to build a society as a family.

2. The God of my people fights for us and I do not suffer

This idea presupposes polytheism. There are many gods. The god of each group protects and takes care of his group. We constantly war with other groups to gain more power, wealth, and influence. I am loyal to my god and my god is loyal to me.

If we scratch under the surface of the wars and conflicts between people of different religions or even between different Christian denominations, we will discover the main ingredients of this conviction.

Active violence against other people can be condoned and even celebrated as an expression of loyalty, radical commitment, and piety to 'a god'. Many give even their lives fighting the opponents who serve other gods. Every fanatic group proudly exhibits this behaviour. Such front-line soldiers of any group feel rejected and as if they have been backstabbed at the suggestion that 'their' god can love other people.

Wars between countries, religious groups, and denominations can never end as long as people share this conviction even if they don't articulate it well.

3. I am just, and I will not suffer till death

This conviction takes life as the time from birth to death and presumes that all scores are settled before the end of the game despite the ups and downs during the game. Though it promotes the importance of virtues, it does not reflect the reality more than any other wishful thinking.

Biblical Job gets children and wealth after his rehabilitation. How many parents live and die today bitterly weeping at their children's graves! Innocent people suffer and die in misery without ever being vindicated and numerous evil doers enjoy luxury and homage even at their funeral.

This entire notion of justice during one's life-time crumbles when tested against simple day to day experience. People feel let down and disillusioned. Some even conclude that virtues do not matter.

4. Live out the number of life-cycles you want but pay for your actions

This mindset squarely keeps people responsible for their actions and holds them accountable. Virtues come to fruition and evil actions backfire. Death is not the end of life but just the end one of its many cycles.

This conviction promotes virtuous living, but one can feel self-righteous and despise others. I am healthy and wealthy because of what I did in the previous life. You are wretched and poor because of your evil in the last life. No room for compassion.

It tolerates injustice and misery too much and for too long. Why make the life better for others since nature itself will balance things with time?

Absolutely no room for forgiveness! Life works like a machine and it knows no exceptions. You reap what you sow.

5. Suffering and death are not normal

As explained earlier, this worldview shows an overall positive approach to life in general. It is also a pleasant wishful way of thinking which does not correspond to the reality we see every day.

Denying death and misfortunes does not remove them from human life. To keep this ideology intact, people scramble to find a scapegoat for every suffering. On the one hand, it makes weaker people more vulnerable to being accused (they are the only ones who will not fight back) and on the other hand, it gives false satisfaction to the entire society. False satisfaction, because everybody knows deep down that this does not solve in any way the real problems that are in fact more complex and bigger. Finding a scapegoat like spreading a carpet over a crack brings a closure to the disturbing sight of a problem without really addressing it.

***

The implications and logical consequences we have examined so far beg for a different view, a different mindset, a *metanoia*.

II. How did Jesus respond to human sufferings and death?

The vision of Jesus clearly comes out from his reaction to various events in life and from his teachings.

Jesus offers fresh perspectives by the way he faces misfortunes in his own life and in that of others and he challenges openly certain traditional convictions.

Events

Accidents and calamities: Newspapers and television channels report non-stop on accidents and deaths. Jesus too gets very disturbing news from various sources. People tell him of Galileans killed by Pilate, most probably in the temple. Certainly, people interpreted the event in so many different ways. Jesus refutes one hidden interpretation and asks the people, "Do you think that because these Galileans suffered in this way, they were worse sinners than all other Galileans?" (Lk 13:2) Jesus talks of the victims as those who *"suffered"* not as those who were "punished for their sins" or those "abandoned by God". Some might have felt that God did not intervene to save them from Pilate because they were from Galilee (the north) and not from Judea where Jerusalem is.

Jesus refers to another calamity that seems to have happened in Jerusalem itself - the fall of the tower of Siloam, killing eighteen people. The mention of this calamity neutralises the superiority of Jerusalem over Galilee. Then in the interpretation, Jesus repeats himself saying that they were not worse sinners than the others.

Notice an important nuance here. Jesus does not deny the general belief that sins bring suffering and at the same time refuses to despise the victims, refuses to conclude that they suffered because they are worse sinners and categorically denies the credit people take for themselves for not suffering like the others. Those who were not killed by Pilate or by the fall of the tower of Siloam have absolutely no reason to congratulate themselves or consider themselves as virtuous.

Sickness: Let us look at two instances that show the attitude of Jesus and those around him when confronted by the sickness of people.

First, the healing of the man born blind. The disciples ask Jesus, "Rabbi, who sinned, this man or his parents, that he was born blind?" (Jn 9:2) This question affirms that the sin of somebody caused the man's blindness and seeks only a precision – whose sin. Responding, Jesus declares, "Neither this man nor his parents sinned".

Second, the healing of a paralytic. While curing him, Jesus tells him, to the shock of Pharisees and Scribes, "Your sins are forgiven" (Lk 5:20-24) before commanding him to get up and go home. Jesus shows a real connection between sin and his condition. Forgiveness and healing become synonymous in the question Jesus asks the Scribes and Pharisees, "Which is easier, to say, 'Your sins are forgiven you,' or to say, 'Stand up and walk'?" (Lk 5:23). The only other place where Jesus says, "Your sins are forgiven" is to the repentant woman who anointed his feet (Lk 7:48).

Jesus does not see suffering as a deserved punishment for a sinner which can make one despise the suffering person and pacify one's own conscience for not offering any support. It is like saying, "It is right and just that you suffer, because you are paying for your sins. I will make sure not to become like you. Thank you for teaching me a lesson". Jesus sees the suffering 'caused' by a sinful life. This little nuance makes a world of difference. When a sinful person realises how much he or she is suffering due to a sinful life, the person desires a change. Conversion of lifestyle becomes not only a hopeful possibility but also the most convenient and sensible option. Forgiveness becomes liberation. Every sin leads to slavery and suffering but every suffering does not come from one's own sins.

In the above instances, Jesus liberates the paralytic and the anointing woman from suffering and sin by declaring forgiveness. The man born blind too has been going through a lot of suffering and Jesus does not link it to any sin. Jesus has compassion for the blind man too, gets into action and offers him a better life.

Death: The Scriptures give us a closer look at the reaction of Jesus to the reality of death in two cases - the son of the widow of Nain and Lazarus. In the first case, neither the dead man nor his mother is named. Probably Jesus did not know them personally. The second is a dear friend of Jesus. We know the name of the dead person and that of his sisters. Both the anonymous person and the dear friend face the same reality - death. Jesus is deeply moved with compassion in both instances! Look at this emotional response of Jesus. He is shaken. In the case of the death of Lazarus, Jesus knew already what he was going to do and that is why he delayed going up to Bethany (Jn 11:4-6). Despite that, when he sees people weeping, he is deeply troubled and weeps.

On both these occasions, we do not see Jesus accusing the dead people or the others for their death. He faces the reality, shares the pain of the bereaved and is deeply moved with compassion.

Life of Christ

Look at the personal life of Christ himself; he does not come under the category of the blessed, privileged people according to the old understanding. He did not own plenty of riches and animals. He did not have a big household. He led the very ordinary life of the majority. In the society where widows stood at the bottom of the ladder, he counted his own mother as one of them. He was a victim of false accusation and assassination. Though he was taunted, 'Save yourself if you are the son of God' (Mt 27:40), he ended up really dying on the cross.

Teachings

We saw the response of Jesus to various situations - accidents, sickness, and death. Some of his reactions shock some and scandalise others. They naturally shake the fundamental conventional convictions. Let us look at his teachings now where he clearly sets out a different paradigm altogether.

God, the father of all, not the leader of an elite club

In the first part we saw the notion of being 'God's people' where god fights against those who want to harm his people. The most important virtue according to this notion is to remain uncontaminated by others and be faithful to the protecting god, by following all that distinguishes them from others. Even at the time of Jesus, the Jews suffered under the Roman occupancy and people prayed so that God would fight their cause against the Romans. Many were praying for a messiah through whom god would free them.

Jesus shatters those dreams and expectations by changing the entire framework. First, he does not consider political change as his mission or priority. Secondly, he talks of God not as the protector of his people against their enemies, but as a father who cares for 'every being'. He feeds the birds of the air who neither sow nor reap (Mt 6:26), "makes his sun rise on the evil and on the good, and sends rain on the righteous and on the unrighteous" (Mt 5:45). If this is the identity of God, then it is not only unimaginable for God to destroy the opponents of the people, but it also becomes an obligation for the disciples to 'love their enemies and pray for those who persecute them' (cf. Mt 5:44). The logic behind all this shows that everybody is a child of God. No more room for a special status, privileges, and entitlements. I can get no favour from God at the expense of others.

What does it mean then to be a disciple of Christ? Jesus asks his disciples to imitate, reflect and resemble God as children imitate, reflect, and resemble their father.

When my bodyguard knows no one in town, he will tear to pieces anyone who harms me. But what if he is closely related to everybody in town including those I do not like? The inclusion of others means dilution of one's entitlement. This notion brings a massive sense of loss and even indignation which we see in the Scribes, Pharisees, the laborers of the first hour (" You have made them equal to us" Mt 20:12) and the elder brother of the prodigal son (Lk 15:30).

Will I be spared from suffering? Certainly not!

Once the idea of god as a personal bodyguard against others, has fallen, there is a desperate question. Will I be spared from suffering? Let us face the blunt answer 'No'. Jesus makes no promise that he would spare us from suffering. On the contrary, he guarantees suffering to his disciples (Mt 24:9-14).

Expect storms and you are empowered to face them

How do you imagine a disciple of Christ - someone wrapped up in a blanket and kept in a bunker during the storm? No, the disciples resemble the house built on a rock which faces the storm fearlessly. It is battered and beaten by winds and floods but stands firm - not without bruises (cf. Mt 7:24-25).

First, Jesus affirms that storms in life, in addition to being unavoidable, are also to be expected and even chosen voluntarily because the easier options we find in life lead to destruction. "For the gate is narrow and the road is hard that leads to life" (Mt 7:13-14). Therefore, the normal everyday life of a disciple resembles passing through a narrow gate.

Secondly, he tells the disciples repeatedly that there is no reason to panic. They are very well empowered to face anything. (Mk 13:11).

Certainly, when people choose the tough option first, they become like resilient soldiers. Apart from the inner strength, confidence, and resilience we build up through this mindset, Jesus promises his direct support when we face storms and battles. The heavenly Father knows our needs (cf. Mt 6:32), listens to our prayers and provides us with all our needs (cf. Jn 16:23-24). The Holy Spirit is with us as a coach and guide (cf. Jn 16:7-13).

The bottom line - 'Do not be afraid of anything. You are well empowered'.

What stunning good news! A totally different sense of security and confidence!

Human beings bring out their best when they feel confident and secure and they bring out their unimaginable worst when they feel threatened and insecure.

Attitude towards those beaten and bruised

Winds will keep blowing and storms will keep hitting. What about the people flat on the ground totally beaten? We see a clear teaching in the parable of the good Samaritan. Pope Francis makes a very interesting observation in the recent encyclical 'Fratelli tutti' saying that the parable begins with a victim and the robbery has already taken place. No crime details to distract us. How are you going to respond? Help the victim on the ground or pass by? (cf. Art 72-74)

Jesus puts compassion and concrete action before everything else. No room for blame games or academic analysis which become often excuses to avoid compassion and action.

Framework of life

For those who saw death as the ultimate loss, Jesus taught his followers not to be afraid of those who can kill only the body (Mt 10:28)! This teaching minimised the fear of death and stressed eternal life. In talking of this, Jesus echoed not the thinking of the books written during the period of conquest, but those written during moments of exile and persecution like the books of Daniel and Maccabees.

We see life as eternal, death as a doorway and the acceptance of suffering as an expression of courage and fidelity. These parameters remain the same even when there is no persecution of one nation by another and even when we realise that all of us make one family.

Apart from hearing the teachings of Jesus, the disciples experienced the glorious risen Christ and the strengthening presence of the Holy Spirit in their lives.

III. Amazing grace

We saw in the first part the human desire not to suffer and how various notions about God supported that desire. Every conviction discussed above surely had certain spiritual experiences at its origin and at the same time, we notice several problems and inconsistencies when we push them beyond a certain limit.

Still today, we come across the different ideas and mental frameworks we discussed in the first section. In the second part we saw how Jesus placed suffering, morality, and consequences of one's actions in the overall framework of life.

In this final section we will keep the baby and throw away only the bathwater. Ideologies evolve only when they are identified, articulated, and challenged. If many religious convictions are based on certain real personal spiritual experiences, we need to carefully analyse the conclusions people have made from those experiences and try to bring out a consistent Christian understanding based on the life and teachings of Jesus Christ.

1. I am special and precious like everybody else

People experience the love, care, and protection of God very clearly at various key moments of their lives. The unmistakable experience overwhelms them with joy and gratitude. The distortion happens when they conclude that the love, they experience is a privilege granted *only* to them, since they are *special*. This changes their attitude towards other people. We need to use with care expressions like 'chosen people' and 'people of God'.

The craving for 'being special' comes from our 'limitedness'. We measure everything and we see everything as limited. Somebody promises me ice cream and I want to know immediately the quantity so that I can plan how many people to invite and they will feel special. Human perception and calculations presuppose that resources are 'limited' and those who are special get a bigger share.

With limited resources, we either dig deep or wide, we either get plenty of cheap articles or a few expensive ones, we either make numerous acquaintances or a few close friends. We naturally think in terms of these mutually excluding possibilities.

God is not limited – a mystery for human understanding!

God can dig wide and deep and can keep quality and quantity together. God can love you deeply and personally and at the same time love everybody else with the same depth without compromising your share of attention.

2. Human suffering and moral judgement

Everybody agrees that people do a lot of both good and bad things. Everybody also agrees that we all suffer. People differ largely in the way they connect suffering to sins and virtues.

Suffering is part of life

Some people naively wish and dream of a life without any hint of discomfort or difficulty. In addition to being childish and unrealistic, such an expectation proves to be even unhealthy. Those who see hardship and suffering as part of life have a greater edge since they are prepared to face challenges and transform them into stepping stones. They bounce back with confidence each time they are hit with something.

We go through pains without any reference to sins and virtues. Hard work, expectation, disappointments, failures, and our natural limitations are some forms and sources of suffering that have nothing to do with sins and virtues. These are essential parts of human life. Therefore, though sins lead to suffering, every suffering is not a consequence of sins. The suffering person is neither a victim of an offence inflicted by someone nor is he a punished offender.

Seeing the man born blind, the disciples of Jesus asked, "Is it because of his sins or those of his parents that he is blind?". We hear so many versions of this question in our everyday life like: "He was such a good man but why does this happen to him? Are we facing this pandemic as a punishment for our sins? Did my favourite football club lose because during the long homily last Sunday I slept?"

Though some of this can help us to improve a certain aspect of our lives, this perspective engenders either a guilt feeling or a resentment towards others. It also distorts the image of God.

Challenges, difficulties, and suffering are part of life. We face them with confidence, we support each other with compassion and keep moving forward.

No impunity

Sin leads to suffering and death. For example, gluttony leads to obesity and heart-attack. Apart from such natural consequences, sins attract suffering from the legal system as they breach social contracts. The one who steals loses his job, goes to prison, and faces several consequences that impact his day-to-day life. Of course some people succeed in dodging the legal system!

Does God intervene to punish sins and when does that happen? How do we understand justice from the teachings of Christ?

Jesus talks clearly of accountability for our life and certainly there is no notion of impunity for anyone. Those who received more will be asked to account for more. Jesus talks of the heavenly Father rewarding those who pray and give alms in secret, teaches about the king who rewards his servants who managed what was entrusted to them. At the same time Jesus talks of weeping and grinding of teeth for those who did not manage what was entrusted to them. Therefore, good actions and bad actions have corresponding pleasant and unpleasant consequences coming from God.

The virtues and vices, even those invisible to the eyes of the society, have their consequences in the wider picture of life that includes life after death. Though the fear of punishment serves as a poor motivational factor to do good, the concept of impunity has enormous potential for evil.

No Karma either but grace

The consequences of our actions are not as mechanical as the idea of karma (fortunately!). We face here the mystery of the amazing grace which leaves room for forgiveness and hope for a better life and a new beginning. No impunity and no Karma. What are we left with?

Justice and mercy.

In other words, accountability, and magnanimity.

Truth and love.

3. Endurance and Providence

One of the most common and at the same time powerful pastoral encounters is the one around a sick person. Some of the sick people for whom we pray get better, some continue the battle with greater inner strength and some die. Almost every pastoral agent has wondered what to pray for in certain situations - ask for healing or strength to bear the pain or the grace to accept the imminent death.

This dilemma exposes another grey area of faith. Does God give us solutions to problems or strength to face them? Do we see him as a doctor in a white coat or as a coach with a whistle?

Praying only for healing and seeing that people do not get well leads to the disillusion of the suffering people and to a sense of failure on the part of the pastoral agents.

Everybody has to die one way or the other. People need enough strength to fight the battle with hope. Prayer makes them resilient. Even Jesus went through the passion and asks us to take up our cross and follow him. We also spoke about the importance of passing through the narrow gate earlier. In that case, prayer is reduced to mere endurance building! It then leads to agnosticism and self-reliance.

In many cases prayer bursts out as the desperate 'cry of a human being for help' like that of Hagar in the desert. She has been chased away, she has no home and no protection. Her only son is about to die in the desert. She cries for help. People experience, like Hagar, God's providence in a divine response to that desperate cry during their most vulnerable moments. The amazing grace holds those falling from the cliff of life and lifts up those the society has dumped aside.

Faith in God does not mean the mere belief in the existence of God. The Devil knows the existence of God with greater certainty than any saint (Cf. James 2:19). Is not faith the confidence and trust in the tender love, caring guidance, and mysterious providence of God?

God strengthens us to be resilient and face tough moments and at the same time God also intervenes to sooth, to heal, and to remove a pain or a burden. Are you thinking in terms of either-or? Can both stay together? Imagine God in a white coat with a whistle!

4. Where is the real party?

God has given us life. Where is it and when do we live it?

If we see life as the time between our birth and death, then some would say that it is better to eat, drink and make merry as much as possible They see suffering as nuisance and death as the biggest disappointment and disaster.

Some believers consider the life after death as the real and main life. As a result, they either despise the present life or do not engage with it fully. They put up with everything that is bad while waiting to enter the perfect world - heaven.

Look at the present life as the real life which continues for eternity after our death with consequences arising from the present life. Get fully involved in the world. Be compassionate, make the world better for everybody and face every challenge on the way. Suffering becomes part of life and death, with all that it involves, becomes a door to the next step.

Conclusion

Truth!
The plain truth.
Pains and storms punctuate life.
You are well empowered but not entitled.
Face life and make it better and joyful for everybody.
We make an inclusive family and not an exclusive club.
God is with us as a Father, coach, and a healer.
Life continues even after death.
Virtues and vices matter.
Prayer works.
Amen.

Spotlight: Mission amidst crisis today

Mission-Inculturation: the Challenge is Renewed

Waldemar Piotr Dziedzina SMA

Understanding inculturation

The very concept of inculturation is not easy to define. Everyone can understand it in different ways. Therefore, for the sake of clarity, we want to remember what the encyclical *Redemptoris Missio* says in no. 52:

"Inculturation "means the intimate transformation of authentic cultural values through their integration in Christianity and the insertion of Christianity in the various human cultures." The process is thus a profound and all-embracing one, which involves the Christian message and also the Church's reflection and practice. But at the same time it is a difficult process, for it must in no way compromise the distinctiveness and integrity of the Christian faith."

We can also refer to the post-synodal exhortation *Ecclesia in Africa* of St. John Paul II, which is extremely important for us missionaries. The Pope says that inculturation has two dimensions: "on the one hand 'the internal transformation of authentic cultural values by their integration into Christianity' and, on the other, 'the insertion of Christianity in the various human cultures' (EA 59).

These texts clearly show that inculturation is a process of creative exchange between a given culture and the Church, which "makes the Gospel incarnate in different cultures and at the same time introduces peoples, together with their cultures, into her own community" (RM 52). Thanks to this process, the Church becomes universal and, at the same time, enriches herself with new forms of expression, she learns to know and to express even better the mystery of Jesus.

Three elements of inculturation

This process shows above all the need to bring the Gospel closer to a culture in order to penetrate and enrich each other. Many theologians note that the Gospel is not presented as a mere revelation but requires appropriate 'cultural clothing'. Hence the three-part diagram of the process of inculturation. It is made up of the local culture represented by the local community, the Gospel and the one sent by the Church. There is a mutual interaction between the one who proclaims the Gospel, the culture and the local community. The task of the one who proclaims the Gospel is to penetrate the local community, and therefore its culture permeates him as well. In practice, it is the disappearance of his own culture, of which he is "a product", and the entry into an unknown culture with the Gospel. The following point of the missionary encyclical quoted above calls and recommends in particular to missionaries from various countries and from various particular Churches to become actively involved in the social and cultural life of those to whom the Church has sent them: "moving beyond their own cultural limitations. Hence, they must learn the language of the place in which they work, become familiar with the most important expressions of the local culture, and discover its values through direct experience" (RM 53). When one considers the fact that the local culture must enrich the Church, the role of the missionary is irreplaceable in the process of inculturation.

Double character

Inculturation begins with listening, but it applies to both parties involved in the process. From this listening dialogue is born. It must be characterized by mutual openness, a proof of overcoming prejudices, intolerance, misunderstandings, suspicions and not by a form of capitulation or irenism[1]. As missionaries, we move a lot, changing regions, countries and even continents. We have probably heard from people things like: "here it is Africa, not Europe, you are in this or that country, forget where you come from, etc." Such words, which might otherwise seem right, are in fact an impenetrable wall. This attitude is a manifestation of the demand to tear out the cultural roots of someone who arrives in another culture, without any openness or empathy on the part of those who live there. Such an approach does not serve dialogue, understanding or mutual trust.

As missionaries *ad gentes*, *ad extra*, *ad vitam*, we are constantly participating in the process of inculturation, whether we like it or not. This process is permanent, because cultures are constantly changing, forcing us to adopt a new approach, which is expressed in the spirit of dialogue. In this way, inculturation will be a process that creates an opportunity to consolidate the presence of Christianity in the world and in cultures and will allow us to prepare for the challenges that the future will present to us.

Adaptation

Inculturation is a process of incorporating the Christian life and the message into a given cultural space. If this process does not lead to changes in the given culture then we cannot speak of inculturation, but only of a superficial adaptation. This is one of the difficulties and threats that weigh on the process of inculturation.

Often, when we talk about inculturation, we are really talking about adaptation. For the process of inculturation to unfold properly, it must not stop at adaptation, but it must go further and deeper. It must reach out to people and communities subject to inculturation. Therefore, it must include all members of a given community. It cannot exclude anyone from this process.

The Incarnation of the Word of God consisted in becoming a member of a concrete community, a community existing in time and space. This directs us to pay particular attention to the solid and in-depth formation of Christians, as our founder, Melchior de Marion Brésillac,

---

[1]Irenism – from Greek ειρήνη - peace, harmony, security. In Christian theology, it is understood as a vision aimed at eliminating denominational divisions and achieving unity by developing the foundations of Christian doctrine in a way that would enable all Christian denominations to adopt it at the cost of doctrinal concessions.

has repeatedly emphasized. It is impossible to carry out the process of inculturation without native Christians who have an adequate knowledge of their own culture. In such a process, faith is not shaped by someone from outside. In this way, the proclamation of the Gospel becomes a critical tool that calls for conversion and to get rid of everything in culture that is opposed to human dignity and freedom.

If inculturation stops at the level of adaptation, there will be neither transformation nor conversion. Without changing the culture, one can only say that the gospel has been adapted, accepted, and absorbed by the culture, but has not developed a deep and strong connection with it. So inculturation did not make progress, it remained only an adaptation. Without developing its principles, it missed a mutual exchange - from the Gospel to culture and from culture to the Gospel.

This process carries the risk of demands, limitations, tensions and resistance, and in the worst case also the risk of syncretism with the religion of the culture that is being evangelized. A certain decentralisation of the Church's authority is also a source of concern. In the process of inculturation, the 'mother churches' are in charge of the local churches. The danger here lies in the fascination induced by inculturation for history and in the strengthening of local authority, triggering cultural and religious imperialism. Without a certain critical eye, there can be a risk of distorting the process of inculturation - alienation from one's own culture or from its ideological appropriation. Inappropriate inculturation will enslave the Gospel, make it a prisoner of this culture.

Laicism

Following the teaching of Pope Benedict XVI, laicism or secularism and with them relativism, are a threat not only to inculturation, but to the faith in general. It should be noted that relativism derives from laicism and follows it. These two tendencies are described by the Pope as dangerous. As an ideology, laicism seeks to secularize truth, values and Christian principles. This approach tries to detach these values from the foundation, that is, from the revelation of God. Its aim is to separate God, who revealed himself in Jesus, from the values of which he is the foundation. This current of thought seeks support in reason, thus relativizing values. For this reason, theology today uses the term "the spirituality of the Swedish table". Everyone chooses the rules that suit him. They are not difficult to follow, they do not change habits and their application depends on the situation. This ideology not only diminishes but categorically rejects the transcendent truth. The revelation of God, and therefore also the Christian faith, is called into question through seemingly rational discussions carried out in many universities, in the media and in the wider public space.

Pope Benedict XVI has identified people and areas that offend tradition, falsifying the word of Christ to deprive the Gospel of truth, because this truth is too demanding and inconvenient for modern man. We see a very strong inclination towards pervasive relativism. This is also present in the area of faith, the truth of which should be regarded as dependent on the historical situation and on the free appreciation of each one. To avoid these attitudes, believers must be vigilant and constantly confront their convictions with the Gospel and with the tradition of the Church. This is of great importance for preaching because the transmission of the integral truth can open to adherence to the crucified and risen Lord for the salvation of all. Modern man needs God who gives meaning to his life.

On the other hand, relativism relativizes everything to such an extent that it is difficult to distinguish good from evil. Man, threatened by laicism and relativism, needs God, Jesus and the community of the Church more than ever. All this can lead him to reconciliation and unity.

The areopagus of the digital continent

This is another threat to the process of inculturation because inculturation cannot be separated from culture. Today we are dealing with cyberculture. The Popes of recent years have been open to discussing the subject of social media. This despite the many risks and dangers caused by the existence of the digital world. Saint John Paul II saw the internet as a tool for evangelisation.

Certain phenomena specific to the digital and virtual world are a real threat to inculturation. Here is *FOMO* (*fear of missing out* - the fear of missing important information) as one example. The *MOMO Challenge* is a phenomenon that police has been warning about for some time. It is a threat to people who use WhatsApp. *FLAMING* (fiery, flaming), a phenomenon related to hate speech and trolling. This is about deliberately triggering discussion in order to arouse strong and negative emotions in other users. These are just a few examples among many.

Many negative phenomena of the virtual world have become a challenge for inculturation. Pope Benedict XVI described all of these social media sites as a digital continent, while Pope Francis clarified the concept in these terms: "The great digital continent not only involves technology, but it is made up of real men and women who bring with them their hopes, their suffering, their concerns and their pursuit of what is true, beautiful and good."[2] Therefore, we can conclude that social networks are spaces for the exchange of thoughts, preferences and points of view. The teaching of the Popes shows a shift from the understanding of the digital continent as a tool to its vision as a space. This change in understanding has also become, along with the many dangers, a challenge to enter into this space with the Gospel.

Emigration

Emigration is not inherently bad. In the Bible we find arguments for and against it. God, choosing Abraham, called him out of his country. It is a specific call not so much to move from a place but a call toward good and toward freedom. The exodus of the Israelites from Egypt can also be seen as an emigration toward liberation. Jesus' command: "Go into the whole world and proclaim the Gospel to every creature" (Mk 16:15), invites you to go out. Being a missionary involves in a way being a migrant. Emigration can also be an exile, a banishment. For centuries, the penalty of exile was considered almost equal to death. Emigration can cause suffering, and this can be seen in the example of exile, deportation or so-called "ethnic cleansing" of any kind.

Excessive immigration creates serious problems for a given country with the admission and integration of newcomers. The contemporary world is becoming smaller and smaller and emigration left to itself is a multifaceted reality that can be dangerous. The migration crisis has opened the space for disinformation activities. The tension and emotions that accompany the problem of migration, along with the possibility of using social media, create a large area of exposure to manipulation. An important factor is the media coverage of terrorist attacks due to new media and modern means of communication, such as social networks, where anyone with an active internet connection is a journalist reporting the incident. For this reason, every terrorist attack is an event of colossal importance. The rank of terrorism in social perception has become the highest. The spectacular terrorist attacks by the Islamic State in Paris, Nice, Brussels, Manchester, London, Barcelona and Berlin have made the migration crisis generally associated with the threat of further

---

[2] POPE FRANCIS, *Address of the Holy Father Francis to the participants in the Plenary Assembly of the Pontifical Council for Social Communications*, (21 September 2013) n. 3.

attacks. Fear does not favour the reception of refugees, and they do not want to assimilate creating their own community and their own world. There is more and more talk of ghettos in big cities in the West. The existence of cultural and religious differences is not unimportant here. This is a huge challenge and a threat to the process of inculturation, as the group of recipients of the Good News becomes too diverse, while the local community most often needs re-evangelisation.

Multiculturalism

The very definition of the term signifies a set of doctrines that respond to the challenge of diversity. Their objective is to establish a social order based on the recognition and separation of the rights of minority groups. This means legal exceptions for various groups (e.g., the right to ritual slaughter of animals for representatives of a Muslim or Jewish minority), the right to limited autonomy, state support for education organized by minorities and finally no policy of forced assimilation.

There is a difference between multiculturalism and pluriculturalism. The latter is an excellent opportunity to see the dignity of the human person and makes it possible to reach an agreement at the international level. For a community to exist, we must know the differences between us so that we can respect each other. If we do not see these differences, there will be no respect. In multiculturalism, the difference is blurred. There is a huge impact of political correctness creeping in there. Excessive mixing of cultures causes given cultures to lose their expressiveness and distinctiveness. The dialogue of cultures, religions and nations is increasingly difficult to see as a means of shaping interpersonal relationships.

Given the conditions conducive to intercultural education, we can distinguish two types of societies: a society favouring the formation of closed attitudes and a society open to the otherness. These types of societies come with two opposing identity models: closed and open. A closed identity is considered to be the property of individuals who generally know little about their identity elements but display a strong emotional connection with them and are strongly attached to them. Discussing about it with them is quite difficult. They are also not very open to accepting elements of a foreign culture. They tend to create and perpetuate stereotypes and prejudices towards others. They treat them like strangers who threaten them. They constitute fertile ground for the formation of ethnocentric and chauvinistic attitudes.

In contrast, attitudes defined as an open identity concern people who are generally familiar with their elements, are able to explain them to others and to discuss about them. They are open to others, easily assimilate their way of life and engage in activities with them without fear of losing their own identity. The greater the acceptance of one's identity and the more complete one's awareness, the greater the openness to others, to others, without fear of losing one's identity. Opening up to the formation of this identity that can be described as dynamic, mature and cohesive, allows to overcome the limits of closed identity that is emotionally unstable, insecure and fearful of its relics.

Multiculturalism is extremely demanding. Mature people with a clear, mature identity, mentally healthy and capable of altruism can engage in it. Its condition is therefore the maturity of the cultures that make up this multiplicity. A person can only create his identity and personality under the conditions of a certain minimal influence of the cultural environment. The threat does not come directly from diversity, but from the lack of micro-culture which makes it possible to respond to this multiplicity, to find one's way around it, and to build, at least, clear horizons of reference. Open identity needs a familiar micro-culture, through which it can properly shape the dynamic and diverse reality of human existence.

Indifferentism

Religious indifference and the development of individualized religiosity challenge the Church more than atheism with its denial of the existence of God. Unlike theoretical atheism, which contains a certain thought and a certain concept of morality, indifferentism is expressed as a total indifference to all objective principles and values. It relativizes them and tries to dismiss the metaphysical questions inherent in the soul and in the human conscience. It treats religion as something of little importance, a superstition or a luxury. Such an attitude is gaining more and more supporters with whom dialogue is almost impossible.

Unfortunately, there is a lot of emphasis on the need to preach the Good News to those who have not had the opportunity to know Jesus, to the detriment of those who have become indifferent. Difficulties in communication are probably the cause. However, the process of inculturation must also include these people in order to be comprehensive and credible. It is a great challenge of modern times.

It is arguably much easier to evangelize those who seek God and are open to his action than those who do not care. The first way to reach these people with the Gospel message is to notice them and to try to build personal relationships. The evangelizing dialogue with an indifferent person must consider his well-being and the truth that concerns him.

In the beginning, this dialogue should not be a pastoral activity. During the first contacts with indifferent people, the overexposure of the religious dimension can provoke their complete closure and even their hostility. In this case, inculturation therefore takes on a somewhat individual character.

Card. Joseph Ratzinger emphasizes that "evangelizing is not merely a way of speaking, but a form of living: living in the listening and giving voice to the Father... This Christological and pneumatological form of evangelisation is also, at the same time, an ecclesiological form: the Lord and the Spirit build the Church, communicate through the Church. The proclamation of Christ, the proclamation of the Kingdom of God presupposes listening to his voice in the voice in the Church"[3]

A threat to inculturation will also be the way of life of those responsible for it, that is, ourselves. This lifestyle should reflect professed faith. Missionaries must remember that to be an instrument of evangelisation in the hand of God, their whole personality must naturally radiate a certainty based on God and on faith.

For this reason, Card. Ratzinger reminds us that the first step is to ensure that God's voice is heard and understood. The goal of the one who proclaims the Gospel is not to put himself in the centre of attention, but to serve the good of a person. It requires from him an attitude of self-denial and of offering himself to Christ in another person.

Card. Ratzinger teaches that we should not speak of inculturation, but of the meeting of cultures. For some, inculturation presupposes a faith devoid of culture, which enters into a religiously indifferent culture, which leads to the meeting of two foreign subjects and their synthesis. According to him, such a meeting is impossible, because faith cannot exist without culture, nor can a culture be devoid of religious elements. On the path to inculturation thus understood, divisions too deep to be overcome create an additional obstacle.

The alienation of man or his indifference is also a threat that hinders his ability to know and separates him from the truth, and therefore from the Gospel which is proclaimed.

---

[3] J. RATZINGER, *Address to catechists and religion teachers* (10 December 2000).

Conclusion

I suggest as a conclusion the prayer taken from the encyclical of Pope Francis *"Fratelli tutti"* (287). May his words encourage us in our efforts, despite the difficulties, for the implantation of the Gospel in new areas of life.

Lord, Father of our human family,
you created all human beings equal in dignity:
pour forth into our hearts a fraternal spirit
and inspire in us a dream of renewed encounter,
dialogue, justice, and peace.
Move us to create healthier societies
and a more dignified world,
a world without hunger, poverty, violence and war.
May our hearts be open
to all the peoples and nations of the earth.
May we recognize the goodness and beauty
that you have sown in each of us,
and thus forge bonds of unity, common projects,
and shared dreams. Amen.

Ivory Coast Political Crisis of 2002

Ramón Bernad SMA

Crisis of 2002

My experience is from September 17, 2002, when the politico-military uprising broke out in Côte d'Ivoire. The country remains divided in two. During the first weeks there was no communication, no news, no transport of people or trade between the two areas. We lost contact with the dioceses, confreres, parishes and the population of Bouaké, Katiola, Korhogo, Odienné, and part of Daloa, Man and Bondoukou. We saw thousands of displaced people arriving in Abidjan from these areas who told of the atrocities suffered and the families of Abidjan welcome them with open arms.

In my office, well installed as parish priest of Saint Bernadette in Marcory, I saw the arrival of former parishioners who told me in what dramatic and tragic conditions they had to leave everything in Bouaké: houses, vehicles, and walk 120 kms to Yamoussoukro. I saw their swollen feet with wounds and heard the story of their march through the undergrowth, hunted down by the rebels.

I felt the fear and the misery of these people and I was moved. Deep inside I heard a voice calling out to me to do something, to come to the aid of these brothers and sisters in need. Together with a few members of our parish CARITAS, we organized two small convoys to Yamoussoukro where thousands of displaced people were in tents. We had rented the minibus from our SMA Seminary in Ebimpé and we brought 300 baguettes of bread, 300 tins of sardines, 300 buckets, 300 mats and as many bars of soap, and medicines for first aid. We were able to bring back to Abidjan 25 women, children and old people who were destitute.

Father Jacques Noirot SMA who was the National Director of CARITAS Côte d'Ivoire invited me to join the Caritas Crisis Committee which was being created and with this small team I was able to make 14 trips beyond the demarcation line: Bouaké, Katiola, Korhogo, Boundiali, Odienné, Vavoua, Man, Danané, Zouhan-Hounien, Toulepleu. Each trip lasted around 5-6 days. We were able to comfort SMA confreres, priests, religious who made the choice to remain in the midst of the suffering and humiliated people. In our convoys we were able to carry out people who were hostages in the rebel zone: bishops, priests and lay people. We were able to channel funds to pay Catholic teachers and other people, to send mail. Hundreds of tons of food were distributed as well as medicines to relieve the suffering of the population.

Inspirations

These trips served to soften the harsh faces of the two belligerents who saw us come and go unharmed. It also served to enhance the Image of the Church engaged in CARITAS and to generate a movement of solidarity from the parishes of the South towards the dioceses of the North which were ravaged by the passage of the rebels.

At the beginning of the conflict, the Church thought of a religious conflict between the Muslim North and the Christian South, but our observations led us to identify it as a political-military conflict. The inter-religious bomb has been defused.

This action was the occasion to launch the idea of creating mobile teams of missionaries. They could be deployed in areas at risk of conflict to help and replace colleagues who live in situations of anguish, fear and danger and give them time to recover their physical and moral health before returning to their old posts. It would be a team of volunteer missionaries, able to live in areas at risk and for a fixed period.

Covid-19 Crisis

The current situation of Corona Virus also challenged us. At the Provincial house of Abobo-Doumé we saw the possibility of helping people who had difficulties protecting themselves against the Corona Virus, we targeted the most deprived part, those who live in common courtyards. With the help of parish CARITAS and REST-COR, we were able to distribute 90 buckets with hydro-alcoholic gels, and 1,200 masks.

This served to relieve, initially, the population and to sensitize them to take hygienic and community protective measures in the face of COVID19.

Conclusion

Faced with these different situations of distress, the Church must always remain in a state of alert, not to look aside, but to see reality in the face, not to shy away, not to remain indifferent, not to be afraid to take the plunge on unknown paths. The Lord will be our guide and our support.

Floods in Nigeria

Anthony Chukwuemeka SMA

All my life I have neither experienced a natural disaster, nor know what people mean by flooding. I could only relate about it with the remnants of water in my street after a heavy downpour, but this was never near to the main reality of the flooding I experienced in 2012. This experience have made me learnt how to appreciate the sufferings of people in areas of the world like Guangzhou, Mumbai, Kolkata and many more local cities in Nigeria including Aboh and Oko both in Delta state Nigeria, where yearly flooding seems to be a new normal.

In Nigeria, the rains are usual at its peak in the months from June to October. Due to this natural phenomena, many places especially water bodies receive fresh water. The Great River Niger would be flooded. Its waters would flow towards every local creek, rivers, ponds and artificial irrigation system. This would help provide fresh habitant for aquatic animals and aid agriculture. There would be more water for the plants and more for animals, pastoral animals included. The raining season is always a blissful season, we have never known the rains to fail; it is for us prove of God's constant Love even when we are unworthy.

In 2012, however the rains came as usual. People were appreciative for the new raining season, accordingly farming activates began. By July, people began to notice the unusual continuous heavy downpour, there was hope that it may soon stop. Eventually it did not. By mid July many inland cities were already grasping for breath due to the increasing water level in their areas. From the south up to the middle belt, the increase in water level was already posing a threat. People were being forced out of their homes due to the flood, we started experiencing causalities.

By August, more than 30,000 thousand people were already displaced. Homes and bridges destroyed. Farms submerged and aquatic life exposed to unfavourable conditions. It was becoming uncontrollable and was soon declared a national disaster. In September the Lagdo Reservoir in Cameroon released water and this added to the problem at hand and the flooding grew without bonds.

In total about 30 out of the 36 states in Nigeria were affected and more than 2 million people were displaced. Most affected were farmers for they could no longer receive the fruits of their labour. It was really a though time; humans, land animals, aquatic animals seem to be running for their dear life in the street of life.

We have never experienced such as a nation so the government tried their best to adopt the best measures to save her people. Many markets were flooded. Schools, churches and other social organisation not spared. Religious institutions found the need to equally collaborate with the government amongst other institutions in handling the disaster. Nearby Churches accommodated displaced persons. They supplied their necessary needs and tried to cheer them up as some of these displaced people were already discouraged due to their great loss.

My parish became a ray of hope to the people living in the area known as Cable point in Asaba, Delta state. The flooding had its banks just a stone throw from the parish. Many people living in that area were, affected and it was the responsibility of the parish to cater for them. The parish community accommodated them. The youths in the parish too were very helpful as we all tried to make them feel at home. Most of these people were Muslims; we all did our best to accommodate all irrespective of your religious orientation. After Masses parishioners were encouraged to be generous to them, this little act of charity would go a long way in sustaining them.

As a parish we sacrificed much of our time and resources to make these displaced people comfortable. We allowed proper religious liberty, good water and security. The youths gave good time to always visit these persons, making sure they were comfortable and encouraging them. We prayed with them and shared interesting life experiences. They joined our Masses and they were made to feel welcomed.

After the disaster we realized that we've gained more which we never expected. With the little we did, a great bond that fostered a stronger inter religious relationship among us even after the disaster was established. The incident made us realize that we all can help no matter our situation. It brought to our knowledge that sacrifice is really giving when you don't have. In this situation we shared the gospel no longer with words, our actions spoke louder than words could have done. At last the disappointment of the flood became a blessing in making stronger inter group relations.

This experience brought to our consciousness that we all can be our brother's keepers. We can always help someone facing great difficulty. During this COVID-19 pandemic we can and should still be our brother's keepers, with our constant communication with them even with our social distancing. We can assure them of our prayers and Love by Phone calls, mails and other means that do not require physical presence. We believe that our prayer is an unquantifiable gift, we can offer it if this is all we can afford. Who knows our prayer, good wishes, show of care and love may be a saving hand to someone drowning in this COVID situation

Mission in the Desert during the Pandemic

Ephraim Kway SMA

Effects of the Covid-19 Pandemic in St. Peter's Parish, Lorugum

St. Peter's Parish, Lorugum is found in Lodwar diocese, Kenya and is located 60Km from Lodwar town. This area is semi desert with very little rain any year and sometimes no rain at all for two consecutive years.

Economic activities

Due to the nature of the climate here most people are pastoralists and keep animals like sheep, goats, camels and donkeys. A few people engage in small scale farming, growing mainly sorghum and millet.

In order to survive we rely on relief food from Caritas Lodwar, the County Government, NGOs and other well-wishers. This kind of help comes once in a while, usually every three to four months to be precise.

Conflict along the borders and animal raids

Turkana County borders Uganda to the West, Ethiopia to the North, South Sudan to the East and West Pokot to the South. For many years this county has experienced killings, attacks, rapes, raids etc. from her neighbours. Many young people have lost their lives in the process of fighting to keep their animals. We are grateful to the Kenyan government which has employed troops and police at some points to reduce all these killings though we still experience outbreaks of violence every now and then and we often lose our church members as a result of these attacks.

The diocese of Lodwar, in collaboration with the Kenya Conference of Catholic Bishops, started a program called *CROSS BORDER EVANGELISATION* in order to spread the message of Christ and Gospel values along the borders to stop all these killings.

Effect of Corona virus in this parish

The Covid19 pandemic caught us completely unawares. Most people come to church to hear the word of God and get much consolation regarding their daily struggle and miseries. It was a big blow for most of us here when the government closed down all places of worship and imposed the night curfew. What we normally do in this parish is we get some little maize or beans and share it with the old, the sick and marginalized people in the villages. Each gets at least a cup of maize or beans. They boil the food with some salt and eat it in order to survive. All these people were then not allowed to come to the parish house or the church for such services and prayers. Many of them were psychologically affected. In the process we lost some people, not as a result of corona virus but due to hunger and psychological related issues.

Church response to the challenges

1. As pastoral agents in this place the first step we took was to remain with the people. We were always available in order to attend to any sick call or burial and also to offer spiritual and psychological support to the people.
2. I organized my catechists to conduct home to home visits in order to identity all those who were very sick so that we could offer them the necessary sacraments to strengthen their hope in the Lord.
3. I worked hand in hand with the diocesan health facility available here in order to visit and attend to all those who needed medical attention. We also encouraged their family members to inform us in case of any severe hunger or sickness. The sisters working in this facility were very cooperative.

4. I was able to contact my SMA brothers in the urban parishes for help. They responded positively by providing us with some food, clothes, sanitizers and hand washing basins.
5. In this parish we have a good relationship with our security officers. I was able to obtain their permission to celebrate the Eucharist and to pray in some families whenever they requested it. We didn't want to deny them the Eucharist but we tried to follow the Ministry of Health guidelines and Covid-19 Protocols.

New pastoral avenues

When the government finally allowed churches and other places of worship to open, we tried our best to adhere to the guidelines given. Sometimes we organized the Eucharist under a tree in order to maintain social distance.

We also did more family visitation, organized more celebrations of the Eucharist and prayers in the small Christian communities and more adoration and rosaries after the Eucharist and other spiritual activities during the week in order to encourage people to pray more and turn more and more to God.

We have also realized the emerging need for counselling and accompaniment that the people want. Sometimes, even with or without enough food, our people feel like they want to talk to someone or to be listened to, and we try to create time for this and even involve a professional counsellor from the convent here.

Results of the response of the Church

The Diocese of Lodwar through Caritas did the following in order to help people during this pandemic;
1. They organized workshops and seminars in order to train all the pastoral agents in the diocese on how to help people to stop the spread of this virus.
2. They appointed a contact person in each parish who was trained and would report immediately if they suspected that somebody was showing some symptoms of the Covid19 virus.
3. Caritas Lodwar was able to get some food from well-wishers and share it among all the parishes. It was the responsibility of each parish to share this food accordingly.

4. PMU and PMC[1] offices in the diocese gave lots of attention to children and youths who were not allowed to attend the Eucharist or gather for singing and choir practice. They were encouraged to follow the Eucharist online where possible, to organize family prayers, individual prayers and one to one sharing of the word of God.

5. I was able to drive deep into the remoter villages to meet those people in our outstations and pray with them, sharing some food, clothes and medicines with those who were not well. People felt better and appreciated that they were being cared for by the church.

Lessons from Corona Virus

It is true that corona virus caught us unaware. The churches were closed unexpectedly. It has been very difficult to run our parish during this time but we have leant a few lessons out of this experience;

1. It is always good to have some savings in the parish account, no matter how little, as it may help in a situation like this in order to continue running the parish.

2. Being a missionary priest I should try to be more mobile and reach out to people in every corner of the parish in order to give them a message of hope.

3. I tried to deepen my faith and trust more in God so that I would become like that house that was built on a strong foundation. No amount of natural forces was able to shake it.

4. It is good to pray more and increase my time with the Lord in meditation, *lectio divina,* adoration and scripture readings.

5. It's always good to work hand in hand with the parish council, the church council, the diocesan branch of Caritas and other agencies so that in situations like this we may work together as a team.

Generally speaking, corona virus has affected the life of everyone to the extent that people come to church with lots of fear. We now have extra work to counsel people and give them the message of hope from the Lord.

May God help our scientists to discover a vaccine against this sickness.

---

[1] PMU – Pontifical Missionary Union, PMC – Pontifical Society of the Holy Childhood

COVID -19, A Path to Conversion

Paulin Kouassi SMA

This year has been a particularly difficult one. We have been really tested physically, morally, and spiritually by the Covid-19 pandemic. Without exaggeration, we can say that the world has become an open tomb for some and an open-air prison for others.

It is in this spirit that we have lived and continue to live the reality of the Covid-19. We started off from the denial of this pandemic, because for many, it was purely an invention linked to various reasons. But very soon we had to face the reality as our loved ones got affected and started dying one after the other. And there, fear took hold of us. Now people try every possible means, from the most imaginative to the most ridiculous.

From the perspective of the Church in general and in Egypt in particular, we have been hit hard with the loss of many of our priests (of all rites) and many Christians. It was a painful experience for many families. It has affected the faith of many seriously. Many even started wondering where God is in all this? Has he abandoned us? What have we done to deserve this curse? Or is it the end of the world?

Despite these doubts and the weakening of faith of some, we were able to bring out with some positive things by observing the behaviour of each other.

This pandemic has brought many of our brothers and sisters back to the Church and brought out some from the lukewarmness of their faith. Though our religious premises were closed, the deep search for God is alive. People flocked to our churches whenever there was a least opportunity for a Mass.

And where very often one had to call people to come to church, it is now they themselves who call in the hope of having a Mass. The church has become for many the only hope and possible remedy.

Many Christians have waken-up to a new understanding to the value of personal prayer. They who used to say, we do not know how to pray! Or even we are very lazy to pray! The fact of the matter is that prayer at home has taken on its full meaning and importance.

Another equally important element is that this pandemic has brought many families closer together. We have become more united, a lady told me. Many rediscover the giftedness and importance of family.

And finally, people have grown in love and live it out in their relationship with each other. We have broken down barriers, we all feel like brothers and sisters. Supporting others has become a natural reflex.

With a broad smile which I will not soon forget, an elderly man said "the Covid-19 has brought me back on the path to God. God is truly alive, he is greater than anything" he concluded in tears.

May God help us as we go through the new waves.

To whom can we go Lord? You have the words of eternal life (Jn 6).

Care for Spiritual and Mental Health as part of Mission during the Pandemic

P. Maria Anthuvan Dominic SMA

"I cannot put into words for you the effect of this double blow to my soul. Moreover, the epidemic – which is the worst in 27 years, as far as people can recall – is not over yet, and almost all the Europeans are perishing. It is not impossible that Fr. Reymond and I will closely follow those we now cry for, and the Sierra Leone mission could be over as soon as it started […]. Whatever may happen, pray that God's holy will may be accomplished in us, through us, and around us. Adieu".

To Mgr. Marion De Brésillac, the death of the two priests was really a shock. He did not know what to make of them or what to do next. He was perplexed about the new mission. His only source of hope was to rely on the providence of God. History is now repeating itself. The whole world has seen the worst pandemic ever. So far, the number of people who have died due to Coronavirus is well over 1,620,654 all over the world and 72,735,019 have been affected so far (worldometer, 14, December, 2020). In the SMA family some members have lost their lives due to this pandemic.

As we all live with anxiety, depression, and agoraphobic behaviour, we can say that the presence of Coronavirus and the changes it has wrought in our daily life are making it particularly challenging. We find ourselves with racing thoughts and with existential crisis: *When will this be over? Will our loved ones and we be protected? How much more will this affect our mission? When will God save us?* The pandemic has challenged some of our core values. It has demoralized our mission and its activities. We constantly ask the staggering questions: *What will we make of all this? Who are we without the projects of our life? Have our values and identity as missionaries changed in the light of the pandemic?*

The current pandemic poses a significant threat to our lives and challenges our sense of well-being. It is a pandemic that affects not only our physical health, but threatens our core mental and emotional well-being. The uncertainty, unpredictability and uncontrollability created by COVID-19 pervade every aspect of our lives.

It is a global crisis that instils fear and massive insecurity and what we previously took for granted as safe is no longer safe. The challenges of the pandemic have the potential to trap us in an endless state of anxiety, panic, and depression. As missionaries, how do we stay resilient amidst this crisis and how do we respond to the crisis positively?

1. Psychological reaction to the pandemic

The Coronavirus pandemic can be stressful and can cause anxiety in all of us. Especially for missionaries who travel from place to place this worldwide phenomenon can bring about endless stress and overwhelming anxiety. The core values of apostolic community life are at stake. The formation houses have to take drastic measures in order to safeguard the values of community life while at the same time implementing very necessary safety measures. Social distancing in the formation houses includes the cancelling of community sports, ensuring that there are not more than 20 members at the same time in any gathering resulting in the cancellation of any activity or liturgical celebration that would entail more than 20 people. Although simpler and shorter forms of liturgical celebrations are still held we hide at times the fear and constant anxiety behind our masks. We experience uncontrolled and pervasive fears in our various formation houses and mission places, particularly about our health and the worry of infecting others. Linked to the pandemic then are certain psychological reactions that result in psychosomatic, physical, behavioural and emotional symptoms.

For instance, there was a cartoon image that went viral. The picture depicted animals wandering freely on the streets while people stay inside the zoo and the animals come to watch them. It was a funny image yet carried a very powerful message. Social isolation related to restrictions and lockdown measures are linked to feelings of uncertainty about the future while boredom and loneliness are directly related to anger, frustration and sufferings linked to quarantine restrictions. Even though everyone is ordered to stay at home the workers still have to be stopped from coming to work and the formation houses or parish communities have to come up with alternative strategies to cope with the current situation. Some of the measures that have to be taken include making changes to activities like cooking, looking after the garden or shopping for groceries because of restricted movements. Or, due to a more limited budget, the amount of meat may be reduced and the menu adapted to whatever is available. As a result, frustration, anger and tension among the members are common emotional and behavioural symptoms that emerge from time to time.

Some of the behavioural symptoms also include a reduced motivation to work and disengagement from religious/spiritual practices. Cognitive functions and decision making are often impaired due to high levels of anxiety and fear. For instance, when one student is tested positive for Coronavirus it creates extreme panic among the students and the formation team. The immediate question for all in the community is what we should do next? Should we all be in quarantine? What is the best course of action? There are two possible ways to react to this kind of scenario. One is panicking to such an extent that it is decided everyone should be sent home and the house closed down and the other extreme is neglecting or downplaying the seriousness of the virus. In both cases, the course of action is extreme and aggravates panic and pervasive anxiety or alexithymia meaning feeling nothing or numbness. A more balanced calm composed course of action is what is most needed during this time of pandemic.

But as new measures are introduced, especially quarantine and its effects on the usual activities, routines or livelihoods, levels of loneliness, depression or harmful alcohol and drug use are also expected to rise. Changes in sleep or eating patterns and difficulty sleeping or concentrating are also seen as some of the behavioural problems.

In order to combat the spread of COVID19, we are transforming every meeting or class into virtual conferences and online classes. Even though it is very cost effective the impact of the evolution of technology and the excessive use of it during the global pandemic is alarming. Some screen time reports on our phone use suggest an increase in the use of social networking activity to 200% in order to stay connected to our loved and dear ones. Although some of the apps like Zoom, G Meet, and

Google classroom have become effective in managing classes and meetings there is high risk of nomophobia behaviour, meaning being addicted to phones. Amidst the pandemic crisis, human-human interaction, face to face connections are at high risk of losing their value whereas the virtual world assumes more importance but at the same time may reduce the effectiveness of learning and human interactions. Students in the formation houses are encouraged to undertake a constant self-check on the use of phones and the internet in order not to fall into the trap of becoming addicted to technology rather than using it with caution.

2. The psychological impact of quarantine

This unprecedented situation related to COVID-19 is clearly demonstrating that individuals are largely emotionally unprepared to face extreme measures of lockdown and quarantine. Students or confreres who are quarantined due to the infection are to be treated with much care and discretion regarding the infections in order to avoid stigma and discrimination. How aware are we of the psychological impacts of quarantine? How can we be best equipped to cope with them? A WHO report cites a higher prevalence of emotional disturbance, depression, stress, mood alterations and irritability, insomnia, post-traumatic stress symptoms, anger and emotional exhaustion among those who have been quarantined. Notably, fear, anger, anxiety and insomnia, confusion, grief and numbness have been identified as additional psychological responses to quarantine. Long-term behavioural changes like vigilant hand washing and avoidance of crowds, as well as a delayed return to normality even many months after the quarantine, were also reported. Thus the quarantine period seems to have important and dysfunctional psychological consequences on the individual's mental health not only in the short-term but even in the long-term period.

Care must be given to those students or confreres who have been in quarantine so that they may not suffer any of the above detected psychological symptoms but rather are helped and supported to have a stress free quarantine. Due to the restricted movements, this year some of the priestly ordinations had to take place not in the places of origin of the candidates rather wherever they found themselves. I witnessed a dramatic and a moving scene of the candidate's family feeling left out during their son's priestly ordination. In a way, the family too was quarantined from their son. The experiences and sentiments of the confreres and students being far away from their loved ones and not being able to go for holidays as planned could bring about feelings of frustration and anger. How do we cope with those feelings?

3. Challenges to evangelisation and missionary activities

Amidst this prevalent widespread pandemic, it is crucial to admit the fact that COVID-19 not only has shaken the people psychologically, socially, and emotionally but also spiritually. Spiritual combat too can take many forms: feelings of anger toward God, a sense of abandonment or of being punished by Him; concerns that this trauma may reflect the work of the devil or demonic forces; doubts about the truth of one's religious faith; questions about ultimate meaning and purpose in life; struggles with living up to one's moral values; We might expect the COVID-19 pandemic to trigger many of these profound religious and existential questions. Social distancing has in a way implied spiritual distancing as well. We find ourselves in a moral dilemma as to how to bring the people to where God is or how to bring God to where people are. Nowadays, with the help of technology, online masses, prayers, recollections and retreats are organized in order to accompany the faithful in their faith journey to remind them that God walks with them and amidst them and they are not abandoned. Yet the following questions pose a real challenge to our mission:

- How do virtual religious activities impact mental health, and are they as effective as their live counterparts?
- What role do prayer and other religious practices play in coping with COVID-19 and how effective is this strategy?
- To what extent do pandemics like COVID-19 intensify or diminish religious beliefs?

4. Protective factors and spiritual wellbeing resources

It is highly important and even crucial that we find healthy, protective and spiritual resources to combat COVID-19. It is evident that religious and spiritual interventions play a crucial role in this public health crisis. The Church has discovered innovative and very modern ways of connecting with people spiritually. For people who have lost their family members and friends, the Church provides counsel, refuge, hope and rejuvenation for those who need it. The COVID-19 crisis calls upon all of us to understand, learn lessons, reflect and reprioritize all aspects of our lives—the physical, the mental and the spiritual. By creating more support groups and creating awareness we can help people to be more resilient. That is the only way to confront not just COVID-19 but also its attendant spiritual challenges.

The Church needs to open her doors to her people in order to communicate appropriate and relevant information on how to combat the pandemic. We need to give them support in order that they can help themselves to cope with any psychosomatic, emotional and behavioural symptoms. Our confreres who are in the most affected parts of the world have to be given online support to help them live through this time of difficulty with our fraternal support.

5. The role of Missionary interventions in times of COVID-19

As missionaries and as carriers of the Good News of Salvation our missionary interventions during this pandemic are ones of waiting in hope, waiting for the coming of the Saviour Jesus Christ who will redeem us all and bring life and light to the entire world. Our missionary intervention should bring people back to the Church to worship the Christ the Saviour like the Magi did, bringing with them not just their gifts, but also their lives, their struggles, their frail humanity and their story of long tedious journeys. Similarly, our missionary intervention should be guided by the Star of Hope to help those who have been traumatized and are still stigmatized with the memories of their infection. Our life should be one of living witness to Christ's promise of coming in power to redeem the world.

Secondly, we should work with renewed strength, zeal and apostolic courage to start all the pastoral activities that have been dormant in a way and to reinforce the ecclesiological values like community worship, faith formation, and Christian Communities.

Thirdly, special care should be given to the most vulnerable and elderly of the society seeking to identify them and administer pastoral and psychological care to those among them who suffer a great deal of loneliness and fear.

The arrival of the vaccines has already brought echoes of moral claims by the Church as the vaccines coming from the United States have some connection to cells that originated in tissue taken from aborted foetuses. We continue to be the voice of the Church urging that the distribution of the vaccines should be impartial and the most vulnerable and the countries having no access to basic primary care should be given priority.

Finally, through our preaching and teaching on various occasions to all categories of the community, we need to begin a process of cognitive restructuring. This means that as our family, traditional and human values and our basic human needs of support, love, belonging, security and acceptance have been threatened we have to build a very strong defence mechanism, a fence around us. We have developed certain cognitive distortions due to this unprecedented situation caused by the pandemic. For instance, feeling insecure, paranoia, excessive fear leading to agoraphobic behaviour, catastrophizing all events and situations are some of the cognitive distortions developed in trying to cope with the pandemic. Cognitive restructuring is a therapeutic technique by way of which we identify and become aware of the thought patterns that are destructive and self-defeating and begin to delete and restructure them in order to live a healthy positive cognition.

Conclusion

Pope Francis in his recent Encyclical Letter entitled *Fratelli Tutti* talks about the pandemic. He writes "A worldwide tragedy like the Covid-19 pandemic momentarily revived the sense that we are a global community, all in the same boat, where one person's problems are the problems of all. Once more we realized that no one is saved alone; we can only be saved together. Amid this storm, the façade of those stereotypes with which we camouflaged our egos, always worrying about appearances, has fallen away, revealing once more the ineluctable and blessed awareness that we are part of one another, that we are brothers and sisters of one another". Pope Francis aims to promote a universal aspiration toward fraternity and social friendship.

Covid-19 pandemic, Francis reveals, has "unexpectedly erupted". But the global health emergency has helped demonstrate that "no one can face life in isolation" and that the time has truly come to "dream, then, as a single human family" in which we are "all brothers and sisters". We can combat this pandemic as one human family. Our recovery as a society from Covid-19 requires the fostering of a genuine and positive culture of love, healing, awareness, understanding and respect.

The Digital Revolution And Traditional Priestly Formation: Challenges And Possibilities

Jonathan Malong SMA

When the diocesan major seminary where our students go for lectures was shut down in mid-March, 2020, following a presidential directive which instructed all tertiary institutes to close down indefinitely, in order to combat the deadly corona virus, it dawned heavily on me that the once clear distinction between the "sacred and the profane", "the spiritual and the secular" was blurred. After all, parishes, retreat houses and other places of worship were all closed alongside restaurants, bars, markets and other public places. I had until that day of the presidential directive thought and believed in the special spiritual character and identity of seminaries, worship centres and formation houses. When there was no consideration regarding "spiritual centres", be it a seminary or a parish community, it was clear that the pandemic crisis was a microcosm of a bigger reality, namely globalism and digital life, which have invaded and are still invading the once "stable", unperturbed traditional priestly formation. The pandemic without any doubt increased our dependence on the computers, the phones, television and other electronic gadgets. More than this, it ushered in an atmosphere of fear and suspicion I have never before experienced in life. For the first time we could not see ourselves as simply human beings or brothers and sisters but as potential carriers of a deadly virus. A simple gesture of handshake, an SMA head to head greeting etc vanished.

Though under the same roof we were far from each other for any physical contact became dangerous. The news from the conventional media and social media only increased the fear and suspicion reigning around. The once rarely heard "online meeting", "online lectures", or the infrequent "online shopping" became the norm overnight. Should we send the seminarians home so as to continue their formation online? It was both a laughable and an unimaginable option given that we were so unprepared for the new reality.

Though life has been in some form of evolution since antiquity, the advent of digital life is shaping lives, cultures and values with a rapidity never experienced before in human history. We are probably witnessing a reality that is still unfolding. This article intends to examine the impact of the digital revolution (in the context of the current crisis) on priestly formation. In the light of the current crisis, ushering in a new normal of "online life", to what extent does it affect the formation of young men to the priesthood or what blessings does it bring into the preparation of future missionary priests?

We propose to approach this study using partially the pastoral method. There shall be a descriptive survey of the historical evolution of priestly formation during some important periods of crisis in the Church, including the current crisis. We shall attempt to do an analysis of some "ugly" moments as well. Finally, from our long survey and analysis, we will suggest some pathways towards living the "new normal" as we cooperate with God in accompanying and preparing future labourers for his vineyard.

Part I: A Historical Overview of Priestly Formation— Kairos in Chaos

Unstructured period: from the cradle in the New Testament to Trent

When the SMA boldly asserts that "the primary goal of formation is to help people grow as 'Disciples of Christ' and to help them help others to do the same[1]," the society aligns itself with a solid tradition which dates back to Christ himself. It is no wonder that the document further affirms

---

[1] Cf. SMA FORMATION COMMISSION, "Our Vision for SMA Formation Today" in *Mission and Dialogue*, SMA Bulletin No. 143, SMA Publications 2015, 61-78.

that, "being rooted in Christ is the starting point of a missionary journey."[2]

At the beginning of His ministry with the call of the disciples, Jesus wanted his collaborators and future successors to be around him or to be in close contact with him so that they would bear lasting fruits (cf. Jn 15). From the Gospels we see Jesus who walks around as a simple preacher but the enigmatic content of His words, character, and deeds compel people to abandon their trades, occupation, and family to be with Him. This was typical of great men of God in His days going back to the Old Testament itself. Willing disciples move together with their Master, they stay where he stays (cf. Jn1:38-39), they eat what he eats (cf. Lk 22:7-16), they learn from him how to pray (Lk 11:1-2), they observe how he talks and relates to people, how he handles crises (cf. Mt 14:22), they observe his behaviour, they ask questions about his teaching and try to be like him in their words, character and deeds. By willing and desiring to be like Jesus and staying with Him, the disciples become like Him. There is little wonder that the earlier disciples were called "Christians" – because they lived like the Christ.

In brief, this form of formation of the disciples was highly unstructured, informal and undefined. However, it was by no means lacking in content, potency or relevance. What was key was the contact and configuration of the disciples to their teacher---being with Him. The disciples had crises too but they knew exactly where the solution was (cf. Mark 4: 35-41).

The Apostles of Jesus would in turn have their own disciples. The NT Epistles furnish us with ample examples of instructions given to such disciples (cf 1Pet 5:1-4). The Catechism of the Catholic Church aptly calls it "Apostolic succession"- passing on not just ecclesiastical authority but a pattern and manner of priestly formation as well.

The Contribution of the Fathers of the Church: The Linking of Priestly Lifestyle and Monastic way of Life

We know very little about the formation of priests before the fourth century. What is indisputable is the enthusiasm and rise in monastic life. Being disenchanted and ashamed of "the worldly lives of certain bishops and priests, who, free from the danger of persecution, became saturated

---

[2] IBIDEM.

by the stain of worldly pursuits in politics and finance,"[3] many people desiring to serve God opted for monastic life. Two great figures who championed the fusion of priestly- monastic lifestyle were Gregory of Nazianzen and Saint John Chrysostom. The latter succeeded the former and continued to advance the course of priestly formation in his well celebrated work: "On the Priesthood." Known for his eloquence, hence, nicknamed "the golden mouth- Chrysostom", the source of his influence over his flock however, was rather his ardent love of the Holy Scriptures and his love for souls. He once asserted : " A single man inflamed with zeal was sufficient to reform a whole people"[4]- In his dialogue with his friend Basil in "On the Priesthood", John Chrysostom exalted the priesthood above monastic life, hence, the need for the greatest amount of faithfulness in the midst of the chaos of the time. John Chrysostom probably had in mind a faithful priest when he said just "a single man" is needed to reform the people. In book III of the same work, he summarised the dignity of the priesthood in this way:

Priests need to be pure as the angels, for the sin of a priest injures many, for which he will be held accountable.

Priests must be detached from money... "A priest must be in the world but not of the world".

Thus, for him, the priest needs to surpass the monk in virtue but by no means should the priest construct a wall around himself: "he must be in the world but not of the world". The place of the priest is therefore not only on some secluded pious mountain but in the chaotic world too. I suppose candidates for the priesthood were trained with this reality in mind.

The Medieval crisis and priestly formation

The Medieval crisis lasted up to the Reformation. Some historians describe it as the "Dark Age" of the Church. In regards to priestly formation, what emanated as signs of hope were the emergence of Cathedral Schools and Scholastic Universities. Centres for priestly studies developed in various cathedrals under the control and guidance of the bishops. In fact, the third Lateran Council resolved that: "the Church of God, being obliged as a good and loving Mother to provide for the spiritual and temporal needs of the poor, wants to provide

---

[3] P. Molac, "Historical Overview of the Evolution of the Formation of Candidates to the Priesthood", *Seminary Journal* 13/3 (2013) 7-19.

[4] Cf. St J. Chrysostom, *Sermon to the People of Antioch* 5,12.

resources for her children deprived of the ability to learn, to read, and progress in study; she directs therefore, that every Cathedral School has a Master and a teacher to instruct free of charge the clerks and poor students."[5]

Even with this crucial effort it is worth noting that "the academic capacities of the average priests were not up to the ministry they needed to perform[6]." This however, does not infer that there was a total lack of trained priests. To the credit of this era we must acknowledge the popularisation of *studia* and *lectio divina,* developed by monks and nuns which then gained widespread usage with the scholastics.

When the implementation of the decrees of the fourth Lateran Council were delayed in many kingdoms, there was an emergence of great charismatic leaders – "the spirituals" who took personal initiatives and developed programs for the formation of priests. Notable among these figures is Pierre de Berulle.

Pierre de Berulle's main concern was to form a well-educated clergy, morally upright and pastorally sensitive and zealous. Part of the objectives of founding the popular French School of Spirituality was to achieve this. Some areas of emphasis for him include, "a sense of God's grandeur and adoration; a relationship with Jesus lived out mainly through his communion with his states […] a great devotion to the Holy Spirit."[7] We see here again, as during the Patristic era, reforms in the midst of chaos. Though the French Revolution would destroy almost everything Christian in France, many priests and missionaries formed in the spirit of French School of Spirituality turned out to be great pious missionaries in the Americas and other parts of the world.

We may posit that in the darkest period in the life of the Church, when universally priestly formation was still mainly unstructured and less defined universally, there were still great initiatives at different levels and by different persons to ensure that the candidates to the priesthood were configured to Christ. There were already also efforts towards uniformity in curriculum and method of supervision. Candidates to the priesthood began living in a single building near the

---

[5] Cf. P. Molac, "A Historical Overview".

[6] Ibidem.

[7] Cf. *Vincentian Encyclopedia, P. de Berulle,*
https://famvin.org/wiki/B%C3%A9rulle,_Pierre_de#The_French_School_of_Spirituality (Accessed on March 2, 2021).

cathedrals. It was the beginning of proper seminary formation which the Council of Trent would usher in.

Structured period: Trent and the formalisation of priestly training

The medieval crises lingered and eventually erupted leading to the Reformation. Clerical abuses were certainly some of them, specifically, "lack of trained priests and the weakening of the confidence of the faithful in the leadership of the Catholic Church"[8]. It is not surprising that one of the major decisions taken at the Council of Trent was to ensure a more structured and wholistic formation of candidates to the priesthood. Indeed, crises are sometimes Kairos. A rigorous approach and attitude to formation of the clergy at a universal level began arguably with the Council of Trent.

Among other things the Council made some important decisions regarding seminaries[9]:

Every Cathedral and Metropolitan Church was obliged to have its own seminary.

Regional seminaries were encouraged where a diocese or dioceses were small or poor.

The Council spelt out a curriculum responding to the needs of its time such as literature, humanities, scripture, dogmatic, moral, pastoral, rubrics.

The efforts made by Trent were shortly to be challenged by State interference during the two centuries that followed. European monarchs grew powerful and, influenced by the ambiance of nationalism, wanted the formation of the clergy with some state regulations. In some cases, they insisted on training priests both in the seminaries and in the universities, a system which lasted up to the 20th century in some places.

From this brief historical overview, we can note that there was never a time in history when the formation of priests was without a challenge or crisis. As seen above, some crises were *kairos* when rigorous reforms and individuals' initiatives salvaged the situation. We saw this with St. Jean Chrysostom in the Patristic era, the Scholastics in the Medieval era, the universal Church at Trent, and other bold initiatives of pious Christians such as Pierre de Berulle.

---

[8] P. MOLAC, "A historical Overview".

[9] Cf. SEMINARY OF CHRIST THE KING, http://sck.ca/priestly-formation/history-of-priestly-formation/ (Accessed on March 2, 2021).

Today we are at the dawn of a serious crisis of another nature, totally unprecedented in history. How we may respond to it in the light of previous experience and what today's ingenuity can offer are our chief concerns in the last two parts of this article.

Part two: The current crisis and priestly formation

The present global pandemic has both a negative and positive impact on traditional formation. On the one hand there is an assault on the seminary structures (its visible and invisible structures) with a forceful attempt to severe efforts made at configuration of candidates to Christ by replacing them with excessive reliance on electronics and gadgets –. On the other hand, there is an abundance of useful resources and information just at a click. This section will evaluate the effects of these two realities on priestly formation.

Formation without borders

The nature of the formation of young people since the advent of the digital revolution can only be described as borderless. Globalism and digital life have no respect for physical or ideological walls or boundaries. It is a world of limitless information with little or no control. Many areas of life in every society today are affected by it including the formation houses.

In 2018, in the Pew Research Centre, some experts shared their experiences of the impact of digital life[10]. One of them described his experience which can resonate with most of us who work under indoors : "We text and email most of our personal communications now, too, rather than speaking by phone or meeting up in person. I email a colleague two office doors down from me rather than arranging a meeting…I also worry that social media like Facebook, Twitter, etc… are increasing social anxiety[11]". If adults and experts can struggle in this manner, then imagine what young people are going through.

---

[10] Cf. Pew Research Centre,
https://www.pewresearch.org/internet/2018/07/03/the-negatives-of-digital-life/ (Accessed on March 2, 2021).
[11] Ibidem.

Strange house fellows

One of the activities I cherished as a seminarian was indoor games played together some evenings. It was a good avenue for bonding as brothers. From my personal experience as a "formator" now, it seems students prefer to spend time on computers or phones. This creates a situation of being together without any real encounter with each other. In a research carried out among young people in Ghana, it was found that the most important reason for using social media among young people is the need for friendship (68 %) followed by the need to learn and discover new things (48 %). Rather than cultivate this friendship through encounters with real people, physically close by, this friendship is instead sought like a mirage in a virtual world often without any possibility of meeting. The Covid-19 protocol with its insistence on social distancing only worsens any possibility of contact and encounter between persons. The consequence is that we end up being strangers under the same roof.

Blinded by addiction

The Pew Research Centre also found that young people spend an average of five hours daily on social media. Sharing his experience, David Ellis PhD (Course Director of the Department of Communication Studies at York University in Toronto) said: "several years ago I walked into my fourth-year class and, in a fit of pique, announced I was confiscating everyone's phone for the entire three hours. I later upped the ante by banning all digital devices in favour of pen and paper. Some unusual revelations have emerged since then – including some happy outcomes from going digital cold turkey. The students in my courses are there to learn about telecom and internet technologies. On the surface, it looks like a perfect match: hyper connected digital natives acquiring more knowledge about digital. If only. The sad truth is they suffer from a serious behavioural addiction that makes it pretty much impossible for them to pay attention to their instructors or classmates [12]".

However, his drastic measures were fruitful. According to him, "At the start of the classes... some even drop out rather than suffer the indignity of being offline for an entire class. Yet to pretty much everyone's surprise, redemption comes to almost everyone. Within a month, I get enthused reactions about how good it feels to be phone

---

[12] IBIDEM.

deprived. Grades go up, along with quality of class discussion. Some students report that this is the first time they have been able to concentrate on the course material. Or it is the only course in which they have learnt something[13]."

This challenge is also experienced in the seminary. The measures he took can be applied in a seminary formation house if the need calls for that. The quality of time, human presence and encounter with God and with each other is grossly affected by digital addiction. Even though the digital life offers limitless opportunities for accessing information and resources from around the world, unlike in the previous centuries when information was scarce and inaccessible in many institutions, today, young people still find it very hard to pick out what is essential for themselves in the midst of limitless information and options. As the rector of a major seminary once exclaimed, "They come to the seminary already formed" or they are in the seminary but not being formed by the seminary programmes but by other things online. Unlike in the early centuries, when the disciples really knew who to sit near so as to be properly mentored, the digital world is totally amoral and offers no one credible choice. In fact, the underpinning philosophy is that all choices are good. In the end young people are left to their fate without being rooted in anything solid. This certainly poses a great challenge to traditional formation whose aim, as we have seen, in every century or crisis, is to configure seminarians to Christ and have them rooted in Christ.

Not completely dark

There is no doubt that the digital revolution has come to stay. For it to be so life changing implies there is something almost indispensable for human existence about it; otherwise, humans would have expelled it like a virus from the system. Some other experts shared some positive experiences of the digital life. For instance, Louis Rosseto, a former editor-in-chief of Wired Magazine put it this way: "Digital technology is so broad today as to encompass almost everything. No product is made today, no person moves today, nothing is collected, analysed or communicated without some 'digital technology' being an integral part of it. That speaks to the overwhelming 'value' of digital technology. It is so useful that in short order it has become an integral part of all our lives.

---

[13] IBIDEM.

That doesn't happen because it makes our lives miserable.[14]" Many other experts speak in like manner. Digital technology touches everything about us.

I can attest strongly that without digital technology, the seminary (where I teach) would not have finished its academic year during the lockdown due to the pandemic. Unable to meet physically in the classrooms for lectures or assessment tests, we resorted to online lectures and even conducted exams online. The results have also been published online. The digital technology was such a tremendous help. However, academic exercises account probably for just 25 % of the whole formation process. The very mention of "online formation of seminarians" scares me. Physical presence is necessary for initial formation. In my opinion, this is part of the limitations of digital technology. In the last segment we propose to analyse briefly what we need to be aware of as we live with the "new normal".

Conclusion: as we cope with the pandemic and the "new normal" or "the grand reset"

Holding to the Christian vision of life

The Digital Technology Revolution is just an improved technique for doing things with more up to date tools. For instance, it certainly helps us to communicate *easily* but not necessarily *better*. What if the tools and techniques themselves become barriers to communication, alienate us from each other etc? Then man must certainly assert his superiority over created things and subject them under his feet and not the other way round.

For Christians life is well ordered. By adhering to the Divine order man attains the plenitude. The Christian vision of life is always this: God the Creator first. He is to be worshipped, adored, listened to and obeyed. This is the believers' compass for life. Like a fish which cannot survive or be separated from the water, Tertullian would say we Christians are "little fishes, after the example of our Fish, Jesus Christ... Nor have we any safety in any way than by permanently abiding in water[15]". For the

---

14 Cf. Pew Research Centre,
https://www.pewresearch.org/internet/2018/07/03/the-positives-of-digital-life/ (Accessed on March 2, 2021).
15 Cf. J. Malong, *Keys to the Sacred: Explaining Some Ancient Christian Symbols*, Magic Print 2014, 2.

early Christians, separation from Christ or God was the same as a fish being out of water. Some Christians in the US reaffirmed this bold statement again this year during their conference[16]: "Christ or Chaos," "God or Nothing" as the wise Cardinal Sara Robert proclaimed in his book[17].

Indeed, there are concerns and there is a need to emphasize this eternal principle because digital life is not only alienating us from each other, as we have seen, but almost separating us from God. A chasm between humans and God is being subtly but forcefully put in place. This is clearly seen as the pandemic unfolds, and our reliance on digital technology increases. Gathering to worship God becomes difficult or impossible in some cases. Believers are advised to "worship online". We all know that online worship is no different than watching a football game on TV. Therefore, no matter how useful any technique can be, we must be vigilant that nothing takes the place of God or comes between us and God. It would be chaos. Physically meeting and worshipping God together is indispensable in my opinion. If it means hiding in the "catacombs" to do this, so be it. It is a matter of life and death.

Experts are not always wrong

In as much as we will continue to use our phones for communication etc, we cannot be strangers under the same roof. The advice of experts such as David Ellis (discussed earlier) can be taken seriously. For instance, instead of sending a text message or a WhatsApp message to a brother next door, it is more beneficial to go and knock and exchange a few pleasantries physically. A cup of coffee together would be a great idea. Not every communication can be expressed with simple text or messages. We miss a lot when we really do not meet at all. Perhaps it is time to assert our identity more strongly than ever as Saint Paul admonishes us, "Do not model your behaviour according to the contemporary world" (Rom 12:2). We simply cannot live like the rest of the world or follow blindly. It is important to discern God's will in every situation. The example of Saint John Chrysostom, which we saw earlier, is another good example. Faced with the crisis of materialism, corruption

---

[16] Conference organized by the editor-in-chief of the Remnant, M. MATT, https://www.cfnews.org.uk/christ-or-chaos-challenging-the-new-world-order/ (Accessed on March 2, 2021).

[17] Cf. R. SARA, *God or Nothing: A Conversation on Faith with Nicola Diat*, Ignatius Press 2015.

and indiscipline during his time, he discerned and rightly concluded that for the survival of the priesthood there was a need to blend priestly formation with monastic life. There was a need to save priestly identity by all means possible from the adverse currents of the time. He did not follow the currents. The result of his initiative still exists today.

We are made for rootedness

The constant and rapid change in everything brought by the digital revolution is a reality we all struggle with. Perhaps young people are more vulnerable than others. Whether one is in a parish set up, handling projects, or whether one is in an administrative house, or in a seminary formation house, young people have one major requirement to help them cope and grow. In brief, the need for mentorship. This involves some honest conversation together, getting encouragement or appreciation, being corrected with love and concern, and most especially giving inspiring example of personal life. All this demands quality presence with God and with each other. This can only be offered by deepening our reliance on the Word of God (as was the case during the Medieval crisis) and the Sacraments. Like the disciples who managed their crisis by running to their Master (Jesus) when their boat was sinking, our Superior General proposes the same solution for us today when he addressed the Society during the peak of the global pandemic. Certainly, "To whom shall we go if not to you oh Lord..." John 6:68.

Where is GOD in COVID-19?

Tim Cullinane SMA

"It was the best of times, it was the worst of times,
it was the age of wisdom, it was the age of foolishness,
it was the epoch of belief, it was the epoch of incredulity,
it was the season of Light, it was the season of Darkness,
it was the spring of hope, it was the winter of despair"
(Charles Dickens: Tale of Two Cities).

The Tale of Two Cities is set in the late 18th century against the background of the French Revolution and speaks to us today as we try to get on with life, against the background of the Covid-19 Revolution. In December 2019, Chinese officials notified the World Health Organisation (WHO) about the outbreak of a previously unknown virus in the city of Wuhan in central China. Since then, cases of the coronavirus, named Covid-19 by the WHO, have been reported in every corner of the globe. The virus has astounded everyone with the speed of its transmission and the globalisation of its impact. As I write at the beginning of December, it has affected 64.5 million people worldwide with over 1.49 million dead from the virus. The figures for Africa are 2.2 million cases of the virus with 53,670 deaths. The virus has changed our whole way of life. Mask wearing, which we formerly associated with polluted cities in Asia, is now compulsory in shops and public transport. Social distancing is the new norm. Travel is limited to essential journeys. There is the closure of shops not selling essential items, of bars and entertainment centres. People, where possible, are encouraged to work from home. Mass gathering are forbidden and visits to the homes of other people are severely restricted. This has a serious effect on the mental and physical health especially of older people and those living alone. Attendance at public Masses, is not allowed or confined to a small number of people. Mass by internet has become the new norm. In some places Churches are open only for private prayer. Visits to hospitals are severely restricted and people die on their own without the support of family and friends. Attendance at funerals is also severely limited. The virus, like he sword of Damocles, hangs over the whole world. It is no respecter of persons, of rich or poor, of religion or colour. We are all equally vulnerable. Like the inhabitants on Noah's Ark, we're locked in and don't know when the flood waters will recede and let us return to new normal ways of living.

Here in SMA House Blackrock Road, Cork, we have been in various degrees of lockdown since the middle of March. Our community is made up of over 40 members in three groups. One group of active, one group is in nursing care, and one group of the over 70s who are counted as vulnerable. The virus has hit us hard with 17 members testing positive for the virus as well as 4 staff, all the with varying degrees of symptoms, some mild, some needing hospitalisation and entry into the ICU unit and one person on a ventilator for three weeks. It would remiss for me not to acknowledge the heroic work done by our staff who stood by us faithfully at this difficult time in spite of dangers posed to their own health and the health of their families. There were three deaths due to Covid in the community with no chance to say farewell and attend their funerals as we would like to. As of now we have been Covid free for many months. We do our best to control the spreading of the virus, in constant vigilance, with sanitising, social distancing, staying at home except for exercise and essential travel and with severe restrictions on visitors.

Against this background, a question immediately arises, "What is the virus saying to us? Or, as Christians, "What is God saying to us through the disruption, pain and even death, that the virus has brought us?" Do we listen to what he is saying to us? Jesus spoke about the importance of reading the signs of the times, "When evening comes, you say, 'It will be fair weather, for the sky is red,' and in the morning, 'today it will be stormy, for the sky is red and overcast.' You know how to interpret the face of the sky, but you cannot interpret the signs of the times" (Matthew 16:2-3). C S Lewis wrote in his book "The Problem of Pain and this is a time of pain for many people, physical and mental. "Pain insists upon being attended to. God whispers to us in our pleasures, speaks in our consciences, but shouts in our pains. It is his megaphone to rouse a deaf world." In a similar vein, there is a book called "The God of Surprises" by the Jesuit Gerry Hughes which was very popular a few years ago. Based on the Ignatian principle of "Finding God in all things" and in this case Covid-19, Hughes challenges us "Look at the facts (Covid-19). The facts are kind and God is in the facts."

Negative effects of the virus

On first sight the facts do not seem to be very kind. In March 2020, in Bergamo in Northern Italy 4,500 died due to coronavirus. Pictures showing military vehicles carrying hundreds of coffins spread all over the world, as people witnessed the tragedy the people of Bergamo were facing and brought home to the world the devastating force of the virus. Before we were struck by the virus, the world seemed to work like a well-oiled machine. The year 2019 came to an end full of economic and financial success in Europe and North America. Then, in the first quarter of 2020, everything changed. In two months hundreds of thousands of people died, many more were infected and the economy that seemed unshakeable was suffocated or at least fell into sharp decline. Major companies faced unprecedented challenges and historic deficits were announced. People who were unable to work during the pandemic risked losing their income and faced possible unemployment if businesses failed. The imposition of social isolation measures have had severe consequences for mental health, particularly for those who live alone, and even more so if they had pre-existing health problems. There was a widespread realisation that the 'normality' we were used to, was very abnormal because it did not provide any security or constitute a reasonable defence against attacks coming from a microscopic being like a simple virus.

Positive effects

However, it has not all been negative. The impact of the virus has made us, or some of us at least, more aware of our limitations and of our mortality. With a little virus holding the world at its mercy, it is dispelling the illusion that we are in control of our lives and that by our own efforts we can make ourselves invulnerable We are being given the same lesson as we did with the downing of the twin towers on Sept 11th 2001. In witnessing this single incident, we went from feeling safe and invulnerable to knowing that we are not able, despite everything we have achieved, to ensure our own safety and the safety of our loved ones. We have been afforded time to question the assumptions underlying our former way of living and to reconsider our own faith and spiritual practice. Many have experienced a slower pace of life with time to discern what is important and what is not important in our former lifestyles. We are left wondering if we need all of the international travelling, high density urban living, habitual shopping and long commutes. For many it is an unexpected chance to rediscover different values and ways of living. Many speak of a renewed sense of family, an appreciation of the power of contact with others and of the simple things in life, like the beauty of nature.

The lockdown has presented the churches with a situation unprecedented in modern times. Places of worship across the country were closed for weeks on end, in some cases even for private prayer. A poll was conducted, in Ireland by the Iona Institute shortly after the country went into full lockdown, on March 28th. One thousand people were people surveyed, with responses to the following questions from all classes of society and from different parts of the country. "Have you prayed more or less or the same as usual during the lockdown? 18% prayed more. 43% said, they don't pray, 37% prayed the same, 2% prayed less. When asked "What did you pray for?" the result was Family 87%, Friends 57% Frontline Services 42% Thanking God 40%, Yourself 30%. When asked to list the positive effects of the lockdown people said: People will value family more 85%, We will value elderly more 75%, we will be more spiritual 31%. In an article in the Tablet, an English Catholic magazine, of November 7th 2020, their Vatican respondent, Christopher Lamb quotes Pope Francis as saying that people are called after the tough test of the pandemic to be truer believers and more authentic Christians and quotes the Pope as saying to people, "Don't turn up for Mass if you don't feel the need of God's mercy and you simply are a Christian parrot who recites the words of the liturgy but doesn't speak to your parents or visit the sick." Will the pandemic lead to a more authentic Church with fewer numbers? Only time will tell.

Towards a more caring society

There are signs of the pandemic, leading to a more caring Society. In his encyclical "Fratelli Tutti" Pope Francis says "In today's world, the sense of belonging to a single human family is fading and the dream of working together for justice and peace seems an outdated utopia. What reigns instead is a cool, comfortable and globalised indifference, born of deep disillusionment concealed behind a deceptive illusion: thinking that we are all-powerful, while failing to realise that we are all in the same boat (30), but that is not the whole story. On the positive side he says, "The recent pandemic enabled us to recognize and appreciate once more all those around us who, in the midst of fear, responded by putting their lives on the line. We began to realize that our lives are interwoven with and sustained by ordinary people valiantly shaping the decisive events of our shared history: doctors, nurses, pharmacists, storekeepers and supermarket workers, cleaning personnel, caretakers, transport workers, men and women working to provide essential services and public safety, volunteers, priests and religious" (No. 54)." The pandemic challenges us to change and to be a more caring Society "Let us admit that, for all the progress we have made, we are still "illiterate" when it comes to accompanying, caring for and supporting the most frail and vulnerable members of our developed societies. We have become accustomed to looking the other way, passing by, ignoring situations until they affect us directly." (No. 64)" The world exists for everyone, because all of us were born with the same dignity. Differences of colour, religion, talent, place of birth or residence, and so many others, cannot be used to justify the privileges of some over the rights of all. As a community, we have an obligation to ensure that every person lives with dignity and has sufficient opportunities for his or her integral development" (118).

In his general audience of August 19th 2020, Pope Francis said: "Many people want to return to normality and resume economic activities. Certainly, but this normality should not include social injustices and the degradation of the environment. The pandemic is a crisis and we do not emerge from a crisis the same as before or we come out of it worse. We must come out of it better to counter social injustices and environmental damage. Today we have an opportunity to build something different. For example, we can nurture an economy of integral development of the poor and not of providing assistance. He goes on to say that this pandemic is a call to conversion, an opportunity to change the structures of the world that allow unjust situations to continue.

Example of Jesus

Writing about Jesus and suffering, the French diplomat and poet, Paul Claudel said, Jesus did not come to explain suffering. Jesus did not come to remove suffering. There was suffering in the world before Jesus came and after he went. What he did was to be with us in our suffering. In his public ministry, Jesus continually sought out those who were sick. "When Jesus saw a person in need, the Gospels tell us that his heart was "moved with pity" and did his best to help them. He is a model for how we are to care for others during this crisis: with hearts moved by pity. As Christians, in a time of pandemic, we can find comfort in knowing that when we pray to Jesus, who is very close to us we are praying to someone who understands us not only because He is divine and knows all things, but because he is human and experienced all things.

Biblical reflection on Covid-19

In an article in Time magazine at the end of March 2020, the Scripture scholar N T Wright says "some people in talking about Covid-19, will tell us why God is doing this to us. A punishment? A warning? A sign? These are knee-jerk reactions in a culture which has embraced rationalism: everything must have an explanation. But supposing it doesn't? What if, after all, there are moments such as T. S. Eliot recognized in the early 1940s, when the only advice is to wait without hope, because we'd be hoping for the wrong thing?" What we need to do, argues Wright is to recover the biblical tradition of Lament. Lament is what happens when people ask, "Why?" and don't get an answer

"At this point," Wright says "The Psalms, the Bible's own hymnbook, come back into their own. "Be gracious to me, Lord," prays the sixth Psalm, "for I am languishing; O Lord, heal me, for my bones are shaking with terror." "Why do you stand far off, O Lord?" asks the 10th Psalm plaintively. "Why do you hide yourself in time of trouble?" And so, it goes on: "How long, O Lord? Will you forget me for ever?" (Psalm 13). And, all the more terrifying because Jesus himself quoted it in his agony on the cross, "My God, my God, why have you forsaken me?" (Psalm 22). Yes, these poems often come out into the light by the end, with a fresh sense of God's presence and hope, not to explain the trouble but to provide reassurance within it. But sometimes they go the other way. Psalm 89 starts off by celebrating God's goodness and promises, and then suddenly switches and declares that it's all gone horribly wrong. And Psalm 88 starts in misery and ends in darkness:

"You have turned my friends and neighbours against me; now darkness is my one companion left."

Wright goes on to say that the mystery of the biblical story is that God also laments. Some Christians like to think of God as above all that, knowing everything, in charge of everything, calm and unaffected by the troubles in his world. That's not the picture we get in the Bible. God was grieved to his heart, Genesis declares, over the violent wickedness of his human creatures. He was devastated when his own bride, the people of Israel, turned away from him. St. Paul speaks of the Holy Spirit "groaning" within us, as we ourselves groan within the pain of the whole creation.

As Christians, Wright says we do not do lament very well. "When I am grieving, Jesus is grieving within me and the Holy Spirit is grieving within me (Romans 8). In dealing with the pandemic, what I try to do is to think and feel my way into the situation of people that I know about around the world: either friends of mine or people I have seen on TV, that are in terminal situations, squalid refugee camps and I pray psalms of lamentation trying to embrace them in the love of God. It is no part of the Christian vocation, then, to be able to explain what's happening and why. In fact, it is part of the Christian vocation not to be able to explain—and to lament instead, from which emerges new wisdom.

In a response to Wright, Andy Davis of the Southern Baptist Theological seminary in Durham in eh USA takes a different view. He says that Wright argues that the Bible has no ultimate answer to this corona virus and rather than try to find an answer in the Bible we should follow the psalmists in hopeless lament. Wright quotes T. S. Eliot: "The only advice is to wait without hope, because we'd be hoping for the wrong thing." But the Bible. Andy Davis writes, was written to give us hope. "Christian hope shines brightest when all earthly hopes flicker and flame out. Better than Eliot, Christians have Scripture, which instructs them in what to hope for. Worldly hopes are often dashed because they aren't rooted in real information about the future, but only in good wishes and sweet dreams. Christians know exactly what to hope for. We've been clearly instructed by God's prophetic Word, and therefore, we should be radiant with hope an unshakable conviction that the future is indescribably bright. "Christ among you, your hope of Glory" (Colossians 1:27).

Davis is right in saying that as Christians we should be radiant in hope, but he is unfair to Wright and to the Psalmist. The psalms of lamentation may begin in lamentation but they usually end in praise and hope, though Psalm 88 is an exception as a person shouts with faith to a God who seems to be deaf to his pleading. Take for example Psalm 22. The first part of the psalm is full of lamentation, "My God, my God, why have you deserted me....strong bulls of Bashan close in on me, their jaws are agape for me, like lions tearing and roaring" but towards the end the mood changes as God responds to his cry, "Entire race of Jacob, glorify him...for he has not disdained the poor man in his poverty...he has answered him when he called. You are the theme of my praise in the Great Assembly." Lamentation is not a mode of prayer that most of us practise as we tend to repress our feelings, especially negative feelings and are reluctant to express them to others or to God.

Hope in the midst of the pandemic

In a time of anxiety and uncertainty with Covid-19, like the sword of Damocles, hanging over our heads, there is a poem by an Irish poet Derek Mahon called "Everything is going to be all right" which has a message of hope. While the poet admits that hardship and mortality are a part of life:

"There will be dying, there will be dying
but there is no need to go into that."

The suffering, the dying is not the whole story. While we do not try to dodge the reality of Covid-19 and its consequences for our lives; other pandemics, The Black Death 1346-1353, The Great Plague of London 1665-1666, The Spanish Flu 1918-1920, when churches in some parts of the world were closed for a whole year, came and went and so will Covid-19 for as the poet says

"The sun rises in spite of everything
and the far cities are beautiful and bright
Everything is going to be all right"

Where is God in this time of pandemic? The answer is, He is everywhere if we have eyes to see:

In the warm smile of an old friend seen virtually, gone and now reunited.

In the tear of a family member who lost a loved one… perhaps their only one.

In the hands of a nurse who left the safety of their home to care for a stranger.

In the resilience of a food store clerk who understands the necessity of food

In the care of a doctor who lives a ministry of hope.

In the words of sacred scripture proclaimed in faith, at a bedside, for the last time.

In the Parent who is fearful at the uncertainty of their child's future.

In the pain of a Homeless Shelter and the people who show us the meaning of trusting in providence.

In the hearts of the people who stood on their porches on Easter to clap for a minute in support of all healthcare workers worldwide

In the fear of an isolated nursing home resident.

In the songs of the birds which herald each new day,

And in the majestic purple primrose peeking from the soil.

God is most certainly here. A God who journeys, heals, and loves us dearly. Amen

(Alex Garvey)

On Christmas day 1939, in a time of fear and uncertainty, at the beginning of the second World War, King George VI of England spoke on BBC radio to offer a message of reassurance to his people. "A New Year is at hand," he said, "We cannot tell what it will bring. If it brings peace, how thankful we shall all be. If it brings us continued struggle we shall remain undaunted." He then went on to quote from Minnie Haskins' poem "The Gate of the Year" (1908):

I said to the man who stood at the Gate of the Year,

'Give me a light that I may tread safely into the unknown.'

And he replied, 'Go out into the darkness, and put your hand into the Hand of God.

That shall be better than light, and safer than a known way.

Thoughts and feelings

The virus gives rise to a variety of thoughts and feelings in all of us: fear, anxiety, worry, sadness, joy, gratitude, hope, despair, turning in on ourselves, reaching out to others, feeling alone, isolated, depressed. We need to question all these thoughts and feelings. Some of these feelings are from God e.g joy at the return a brother after weeks in the Intensive Care Unit (ICU), others not from God e.g over anxiety that turns us in on ourselves as if we were alone in the world and the future dark and bleak, without any real sense of God's presence with us in the pandemic." We have choices to make either to listen to the thoughts and feelings that come from God and lift us up or listen to thoughts and feelings that do not come from God and bring us down. A good test of thoughts and feelings is, "Does this thought or feeling bring me peace of mind and move me towards God and other people?" If it does, it is likely to come from God.

As I write this, at the beginning of December, I look out through the window of my room, the trees are bare, no birds are singing from their branches, the ground is frozen with an early frost, and darkness is enveloping the landscape, reflecting my mood at various time since an unwelcome visitor, Covid-19, entered our House. A number of us were victims of the virus but everyone was affected in some way but that is not the whole story. Nature and the trees that I can see from my window are a great teacher. Spring will come in a few months' time with the days getting longer, the trees will come alive with leaves, with birds will sing from their branches and positive news about a vaccine for the virus early in the New Year. Our faith, as well as nature, tells us that after the winter of the virus, a post virus spring will come and as the Derek Mahon puts it, "Everything is going to be all right." In the meantime, what we have to do is wait silently, adhering to the advice coming from Government and the Health Authorities and sustained by prayer, care for each other and the word of God:

"Listen to me faint hearts,
Who feel far from victory
I bring my victory near, already it is close
My salvation will not be late"
(Isaiah 46:12).

Writings of SMA confreres

J. BONFILS, Etre avec Lui. Le pretre, consacré et Pasteur, Parole et silence 2020

B. BOUCHEIX, Monseigneur Boucheix, Créer 2021

D. CORRIGAN, Dromantine through the year. Its seasonal beauty photographed, SMA Publications 2020

D. DISSOU, L'autoconscience de soi et la responsabilité de l'etre-dans-le-monde chez J. de Finance. Licentiate thesis in Philosophy, Pontifical Gregorian University, Rome 2020

M. GUETOU, The divine plan of savation an human response. Licentiate thesis in Scripture at the Pontifical Biblical Institute, Rome 2020

J.-M. GUILLAUME, Bernard Bardouillet sma, 2020

J.-M. GUILLAUME, La SMA en Inde, 2020

J.-M. GUILLAUME, Les Actes des Apotres. Introduction et commentaire, 2020

J.-M. GUILLAUME, Marc, Paulines 2020

R. MANDIROLA, La gioia di seguirti. Lettura meditata della Lettera ai Filippesi, EDB 2020

A. MANDONICO, Mio Dio come sei buono. La vita e il messaggio di Charles de Foucauld, LEV 2020

P. MCCAWILLE, Leaving a legacy in Lagos, OLREC 2021

P. SAULNIER, 60 ans de vie missionnaire, SMA publications 2020

B. SEMPLICIO, A l'écoute d'une retraite, Erga 2020

B. SEMPLICIO, Mgr de Marion Brésillac fondateur "de fait" de la SMA, 2020

SMA TEAM, The life of M. de Marion Brésillac, SMA 2020

L. SNIDER, Discepoli missionari. esperienza spirituale e progetto di riforma in "Ecole apostolique" di Mons. paul Pellet, sma (1859-1914), Licentiate thesis in Spiritual Theology, Triveneto - Padova 2020

X. VINCENT, Questions anthropologiques liées à la prise en charge des maladesémentaux en pays baatonu (nord Benin). Etude à partir du centre psychiatrique saint Camille de Djougou. Licentiate thesis in Anthropology, EHESS Paris 2020

SMA resources

Many people wonder where to find various SMA resources. Here we give them all in one place :

Website : www.smainternational.info

Facebook : https://www.facebook.com/smamediacenter

Our Videos on YouTube: www.youtube.com/smaollywood

Our Photo archives: http://joomeo.com/sma.mediacenter

Contact your Unit leadership for username and password to access over 75,000 photographs.

SMAnetFamily :

- You can find the SMA database including ETAT and Necrology online here. You can also see the list of people who have passed through every SMA address.

- SMAnetFamily hosts official SMA documents that are not available in the public domain like various directories.

- We do online elections through this platform.

- Temporary and Permanent SMA members have received their usernames and passwords to access this cyberspace. Every Unit leadership is responsible to keep up to date the details concerning the Unit. Anyone who needs help can contact the Unit leaders concerned and Unit leaders can contact the Media Centre.

SMA Publications :

Writings of and on our Founder :

In PDF format : All writings of the Founder and a good number of writings on him are availabel for download from our website.

ebook : All wrtings of the founder are available in most ebook-stores including amazon, iBooks, Kobo and Smashwords.

Other writings of our confreres : We have published over eighty books through amazon. Go to any amazon website and search for 'SMA Publications' to access our books.

Printed in Great Britain
by Amazon